SURRENDER

❀

Your Way to
Spiritual Health and Freedom

Mary Hynes, Ph.D.

ST. ANTHONY MESSENGER PRESS

Cincinnati, Ohio

Excerpts from *Yes*, by Ann Kiemel Anderson, copyright ©1978,
Tyndale House Publishers Inc., are used by
permission of the author.

Cover painting, *Morning Song*, copyright ©1992 by Lee Lawson
Cover design by Doug Klocke/Photonics Graphics
Book design by Mary Alfieri
Electronic pagination and format by Sandy L. Digman

ISBN 0-86716-222-8

Published by St. Anthony Messenger Press
Printed in the U.S.A.

DEDICATION

To *MARY and JERRY WULLER*
and BARBARA DRUHE
with gratitude and love

CONTENTS

❧

ACKNOWLEDGMENTS

*My deepest appreciation and acknowledgments
go to the following people without whom
this book would not have been written
and my life would be much less rich:*

Peggy Culbertson,
Carol Falkner,
Terese Ellias,
the Oblates,
Anthony DeMello,
Pam Schaeffer,
Patricia Miller,
Richard Schebera,
Linda Brocar,
Robert Kaletta,
Barbara Bartocci,
Richard Everding,
Norma Putz,
Burt and
  Barbara Dunevitz,
Lisa Everette,
my family,
and
the staff of St. Anthony Messenger Press.

PREFACE

❀

For me, the most exciting and comforting thing about the teachings of Christianity is that there is such a thing as resurrection. Not only the resurrection of Jesus in the Gospel story but resurrections of all kinds throughout our lives. We can experience the death of a relationship only to find resurrection in a more profound relationship. Human life is full of many kinds of deaths and, potentially, resurrections. Although we may not always use the traditional Christian language, we are living in an era when resurrection is a major focus. Self-help movements, national speakers, infomercials and self-improvement teachers are overwhelming us with a kind of resurrection philosophy: "You can achieve whatever you want!," "You can overcome any adversity," "If you think it (success, love, money) it will come to you!"

I believe there is a lot of insight in such so-called "New Thought" messages. I think most of them point to the possibility of resurrection in life. What troubles me is that they do not always tell the rest of the story—the painful process that leads to resurrection. It is easy to see the pain in the life and death of Jesus: the agony in the garden, the crucifixion and the total surrender which comes before the resurrection. It can be more difficult to see how it is present in our own lives, and necessary, if we are to experience the same rebirth.

If it were up to me I would leave the agonies and cruci-fixions out of our lives. But in different ways, to different degrees, they are real and present to each of us. Our task is to look beyond that pain and realize that resurrection is possible. We can overcome adversity. We can achieve. We can love. But we *cannot* control others or all of the circum-stances of our lives.

Despite our best efforts and our most positive thoughts, at times we all suffer. Children are stricken with cancer, people are painfully rejected, homes and lifetimes of mem-ories are destroyed by fire, cruelty and abuse are common-place. The good news is not that we can control all of these things, but that we can live in peace, love and even joy despite them. All of the "New Thought" in the world can-not promise you will not suffer. But every major religion—including Christianity and its profound story of the death and resurrection of Jesus—assures us that we can rise above our suffering. We may suffer but we need not live in misery: There is a way out. It is called surrender.

Watching people try to claim resurrection without going through the process of surrender can be painful. It is just as unreasonable as trying to think yourself into top physical shape without exercising. Organized religions and some individuals have, at times, presented the concept of surrender in a neurotic or emotionally violent way. It is no wonder that the concept has fallen out of popularity in cer-tain religious and spiritual circles. Yet surrender remains part of the spiritual journey whether it is popular or not.

When looking for positive, healthy approaches to the spiritual journey it is necessary to include the principle of surrender. We need only exclude the unhealthy and harm-ful ways it has been understood at times in the past.

Surrender can be a profound and transformative gift in our lives. It can free us from misery. It leads us to resurrec-tions of all kinds. For those interested in the spiritual path, for those who long for peace or love or emotional freedom, surrender is something to embrace, not avoid. Authentic surrender is truly the path to spiritual health and freedom.

INTRODUCTION

---❦---

As I have given workshops and retreats in the last several years, I have noticed an increasingly common habit among some retreat center staff. Before the program speaker begins, a staff member will often address the "retreatants" (workshop participants) and ask them to list their expectations of the program. A form is often passed out for the participants to use. This form will be matched and analyzed with another form, handed out at the end of the program, asking if their expectations were met.

A number of times when presenting a program on surrender, I have asked the staff if they could omit the expectation forms given out before the program. I felt the topic of "surrender" should begin with one of its most important elements—letting go of expectations. My request has never been honored. It has been met with everything from a stern "no," to a polite explanation that there can be no exceptions to the format of their workshop preparation. So, once the staff has asked all my retreat participants to list their expectations, I usually begin by asking the participants to surrender all of their expectations for the program!

This experience has made me aware of just how unfashionable the concept of surrender has become; in some cases, it has been lost altogether. Even those working to guide others' spiritual growth, as in this case, seem to have left surrender out of the equation.

Considering some of the severe and unhealthy ways surrender has been interpreted at times in Christian history, it is little wonder that in our age of focus on emotional health, surrender seems to have been reduced to liturgical song lyrics and prayers at the vow ceremonies of those making commitments to God through life in religious communities.

Certainly there have been interpretations of surrender that have been emotionally violent and neurotic. Good and well-meaning people have passed on concepts of the religious surrender that have guided spiritual pilgrims away from the truth, strength and personal freedom that are at the heart of authentic spiritual surrender. Although the message of healthy surrender has, at times, been lost in fear and rigid theological interpretations, surrender is the underlying principle of every major world religion—including Christianity.

Hinduism, Buddhism, Islam, Judaism and Christianity all call the individual who seeks spiritual maturity to enter a life of surrender. The spiritual seeker is called to give up dependence on material things, dependence on other people, even extreme self-dependence, to God. Even Buddhism, which is technically a non-theistic religion, calls the individual who would walk the Buddhist path, to surrender all desires, all that one clings to.

I spent years studying spirituality and theology before it occurred to me that, while I was familiar with the concept of surrender in Christianity, I had not truly integrated the concept into my life. Surrender was the basis of the theology of Teresa of Avila, Ignatius of Loyola, Francis of Assisi, Dietrich Bonhoeffer and so many others. It was a constant theme in liturgical music. And even though it was the theme of every spiritual classic I had ever read, curiously, spending time talking about turning everything over to God seemed to be the domain of those in twelve-step programs, Protestant fundamentalists or some of those who joined religious communities. In my religious circles, personal surrender simply was not talked about.

As I grew more convinced of the significance of surrender in my own spiritual journey, I also began to spend time sorting through the varied interpretations of surrender and how it might be expressed. Observing the way surrender has been interpreted has led me on a fascinating trip through tragic stories of those who believed doing violence to themselves was a valid practice of religious surrender, to joyous stories of those who experienced freedom from emotional bondage and those who experienced personal resurrections of all kinds. I noted that the resurrections were always preceded by a surrender on the part of the spiritual pilgrim.

In the midst of my theological study, I found myself painfully immersed in what is commonly referred to as a "crisis of faith." It was a distressing time and I decided to seek the advice of one of my professors. The curriculum of the theology department where I studied focused on the academic discipline of theology rather than its pastoral element and, though there were a few professors who had pastoral as well as academic training, I found myself confiding in one who did not.

I explained the pain of no longer knowing what, or even if, I believed. I told him I had done everything I could think of to try to make my faith return. I asked him if he knew of any books that would help, or if he knew of any spiritual directors I could speak to. I thought perhaps he would suggest some writings from one of the spiritual masters or one of the medieval mystics. I wanted him to suggest something, anything, that would jump-start my atrophied faith. I waited and listened. "Ah, why don't you forget all of this stuff and go have a pizza and some beer with your friends," was his response. I was horrified. I had poured out the longing of my soul to this man and he responded with a sarcastic joke. Now, on top of the injury of the faith crisis there was the insult of this attitude.

I have thought about that pizza-and-beer comment many times over the years, but my perspective has changed immensely. Although my professor's lack of pastoral training is still obvious, I now see that his suggestion was basically sound. I now understand "pizza and beer" to be his way of recommending that I surrender the questions that were haunting me and causing such distress and go spend some pleasant time living in the present moment with friends. Now I realize that in order for me to have let go of my issues and concerns long enough to go have pizza with friends, I would have had to have stopped trying to be in control of the problem for at least as long as it would have taken to go out. That would have been a first step to the spiritual surrender which held the answers to my distress.

Looking back, I think he understood that my misery was caused more by my attempts to control my faith than by the faith crisis itself. I have come to realize that learning to let go of control and surrendering everything to God can mean the difference between the suffering that we all encounter as human beings and abject misery, which we need not experience. Surrender is the difference between bearable suffering and unbearable misery. Had I been able to surrender my faith issues I would have still suffered from the loss and confusion, but I would not have been in such inconsolable misery.

At the time of my faith crisis I was not only immersed in the study of the great masters of the Judeo/Christian spiritual life, but I was earning excellent grades on papers and tests concerning the lives and thoughts of many of the most significant thinkers, saints and writers in history. But I hadn't really understood.

Along with the strictly academic work of numerous theologians, I read the lives and work of many teachers of the spiritual life, such as Teresa of Avila, John of the Cross, Francis of Assisi, Julian of Norwich, Dietrich Bonhoeffer, Thomas Merton and Dorothy Day. While I was perfectly able to summarize and discuss at length the works of such teachers, I was unaware that I had not even begun to internalize the message each conveyed in a unique way. At the root of Teresa of Avila's mysticism and Church reform was a surrender to God. At the root of Dietrich Bonhoeffer's sermons on the cost of discipleship, as well as his own ability to pay that cost with grace, was a commitment to surrender to God. It is clear to me now that surrender is the foundational principle of the lives of each and every spiritual master—indeed, it is the foundation of the life of any converted, committed Christian or deeply spiritual person. It is difficult to imagine how I missed such an obvious message.

Perhaps it was the competitive atmosphere of the academic world that allowed me to focus on the works of spiritual teachers without getting the message, or perhaps it was simply my own immaturity. In any event, the message became quite clear one day when a friend gave me a most non-theological, unacademic book written by an evangelical Christian, Ann Kiemel Anderson. The name of the book was *Yes*. At first glance I found the book annoying because Anderson used no capital letters and often wrote incomplete sentences followed by "..." for emphasis. I made a sarcastic remark to my friend asking if Ann Kiemel Anderson was the e. e. cummings of the evangelical world. My joke wasn't appreciated and "Just read it!" was the response I got. I read it.

In her short, simple book Kiemel Anderson begins with the assumption that the committed Christian life rests on complete surrender to the ways of God: finding a way to say yes to whatever God may ask. Recounting many of her experiences with loneliness, temptation, pain, guilt and fear, she simply tells the story of her own struggles to say yes. In one story, after visiting her neighbor and her new baby, Ann ran back to her apartment in tears because she so longed to be married and have a baby. She wrote:

> a few nights ago, i lay across the bed in my apartment,
> and i prayed with all the earnestness in me: "God, more
> than anything in my life, i want to be yours. whatever
> that means. wherever it leads me. whichever things i
> must relinquish. anywhere...anytime...Jesus, show me."
> and i meant it. i have never been more sincere. clad in a
> flannel gown...my hair pulled in a ponytail... I lay there

and waited for God to tell me something dramatic and
noble.

After her prayer, she thought of "great" Christians who had
responded to the call of God—Mother Teresa, Martin
Luther King, Brother Andrew and others who had changed
their world, risked their lives, giving everything for others.
Wanting God to give her a "noble plan" she accepted it
when "in a very quiet way, [God] seemed to say: "ann My
will for you is that you be whole. that you keep me Lord of
your total being. that you learn to be content and happy ...“
    Later, Ann prayed in surrender:

> i stand before Christ and the world. my heart shouts an
> affirmation: Jesus i am a humble, lowly servant woman.
> Take me...all of me. add anything. take anything away.
> at any cost. with any price. make me yours...
> completely...wholly.... May i be known for loving
> you...for carrying a dream...for building bridges to the
> hurt and broken and lost in this world. make me what
> you would be if you lived in person where i do. may
> everything accomplished through my simple life bring
> honor and glory to you. take my human failures and
> flaws and use them to remind those who know me that
> only you are God, and i will always just be ann. amen.
> amen.

From that foundation Kiemel Anderson found her way to
"yes" when she faced the everyday situations of her life. If
she believed something was truly the will of God she surrendered to it even when, given a choice, she would have
written the script quite differently.
    I am not sure what it was about Ann Kiemel
Anderson's book that made it the floodlight on the spiritual life it was for me. I suspect it was the simplicity and the
contemporary everydayness of her experiences. After saying my own yes to understanding that surrender was a
missing piece in my spiritual quest, I began to see the message of surrender everywhere. I saw it in the lives and writing of every spiritual teacher I had ever studied. I saw it in
every book of the Bible. I saw it in the lives of people who

knew peace. I saw it missing in the lives of people who clutched on to bitterness and age-old anger like a security blanket. What was of particular interest to me was the fact that it did not matter if individuals were religious or not; surrender, as I began to understand it, still seemed to determine the inner peace people enjoyed.

I began to notice that surrender played a key role in the lives of people from every religious tradition. I am a great fan of biographies and autobiographies. I realized one afternoon that the most recent biographies I had read had been about people from very different religious traditions. Martin Luther King, a Baptist, was said to have anxiety attacks before he spoke to large crowds—apparently because he sensed the danger in his commitment to racial justice. His friends noted that, at times, he could be heard praying at the kitchen table and surrendering himself to God. After his prayers, he would go and speak as we all remember him—strong and passionately committed to his cause and his God.

Joni Ereakson Tada, an evangelical Christian, was injured in a diving accident as a teenager and rendered a quadriplegic. She wrote several books talking about her depression, anger and frustration—and eventual peace and happiness. She found her happiness, despite the fact that she could not comb her own hair or take care of any of her personal needs, through total surrender. Although, like anyone, Joni has her good days and bad days, she is most genuinely a happy person in a world that seems to expect not only strong healthy bodies as a requirement for happiness but beautiful ones as well.

Mahatma Ghandi, a Hindu, taught the world important lessons about political nonviolence as well as inner peace. He was a great example of one who surrendered himself completely to God and to love.

I also read the autobiography of the movie legend from the thirties, Frances Farmer. She spent most of her life as an atheist. She had what can only be described as a painful and tragic life: She spent many years in the worst kind of mental institutions, suffered from alcoholism and a near lifetime of severe emotional violence from her mother. At the end of her life, after scraping through one tragedy after another, she surrendered to the God she so adamantly refused to believe in and converted to Catholicism. Even after her first experience of going to confession proved to be traumatic (due to the comments of the priest), she continued her commitment to surrender and talked about feeling peace for the first time in her life. She noted that her surrender was to God, not to any particular priest, and once she surrendered she was not going to take it back. I find it particularly interesting that, though I read several books about her and saw two film versions of her life, the only mention of her conversion was in her own autobiography. I wonder what that says about our society and its understanding of surrender and inner peace.

Cesar Chavez described himself to me as a conservative Catholic. He changed life for many of our nation's farm workers and suffered through enormous pressure and character assaults. He explained his inner peace and his lack of bitterness by his daily ritual of several hours of prayer each morning and evening. He surrendered his life and his work to God every day before he did anything else.

I was overwhelmed by these people and their lives for many reasons, but the common thread of surrender was the most influential of all. Given their very different religious and cultural backgrounds, they may seem to have little in common, but they are all great teachers of the necessity and value of surrender in the spiritual life.

Perhaps the most important aspect of surrender I began to notice was that the healthy surrender of people who knew peace was not pious, groveling or defeated. It was not a result of religious guilt or indoctrination. It was always based on honesty and truth and was directed toward emotional, psychological and spiritual health.

It is difficult to think about the many people who have been given guilt-ridden, psychologically unsound concepts of surrender. There are a number of stories of religious people harmed by well-intentioned, but unhealthy, interpretations of surrender. Here are a few I have heard while giving surrender workshops:

❀ An elderly woman who was a gifted pianist as an adolescent was told to surrender her piano playing—and any "unholy" feelings of "specialness" it gave her—as a gift to God.

❀ Some people were told that their grief was selfish and unholy, and that God demanded they surrender it.

❀ Some were told to ignore their anger—not to express it, but to surrender it to God and put on a smile.

❀ One woman was still in a state of shock after finding out that her husband of many years had betrayed her, when her church friends began quoting forgiveness Scriptures to her and instructed her to surrender the hurt she felt to the Lord and forgive her husband—immediately!

❀ Countless people have been advised to keep their stories of abuse quiet for "the good of others." They were told to offer it up to God, to surrender it, to let go and forgive, without any mention of the long, complex process often necessary for such forgiveness to occur.

I truly grieve when considering how many times people have been told (by those who believed they were spreading the message of religious surrender), not to acknowledge their pain, their honest feelings or the truth of a situation in the name of surrendering to God. It is no wonder that the mention of the concept of surrender creates discomfort for many people who have interpreted it, or had it interpreted for them, in emotionally violent ways.

The idea of surrender can be damaged simply by the way it is presented. Thinking back to the "pizza and beer" discussion with my theology professor, although I believe his message was sound, his delivery was flawed. Even if I had understood the importance of surrender at that time, a terse quip, however well-intentioned, would have done nothing to guide me toward being able to surrender.

How is it possible that in this post-psychology, self-help, self-improvement world we live in, we still have many people who assume that giving the command to "let go!" or "surrender!" can simply be followed with no consideration given to the *process*? It is the lack of understanding of this process and the individual amounts of time it can take that can contribute to the horror stories some people associate with the concept of surrender. Understanding that surrender can only be authentically attained when you are truly ready and open to surrender, *not* when your friends or family think it is time, is an important first step to living the spiritual surrender.

Once we recognize that surrender has its own timetable, and decide not to try to force surrender on ourselves or others, we are free to explore, pressure-free, what the authentic religious surrender means for each one of us.

How does one reconcile the concept of a perfectly loving God with the concept of surrender? Are the two concepts mutually exclusive? Exactly what is the Judeo/Christian concept of surrender and how do we distinguish healthy from unhealthy interpretations of it?

These are questions I have grappled with for years and this book, the result of my ongoing investigation of the concept of surrender, offers some of the insights I have gained through my search. My search continues, as does the struggle to implement surrender in my life. I know that it is a lifelong process. But, having been freed of some of the misery that clutching and clinging creates has made me a true believer in Saint Paul's contention that it is possible, regardless of circumstances, to experience a peace that is beyond all human understanding.

CHAPTER ONE

———————— ✿ ————————

Defining Surrender

"The great act of faith is when
[we] decide [we are] not God."

— OLIVER WENDELL HOLMES

Surrender, most simply put, is the living out of the recognition that we are not God. Perhaps that definition sounds strange—surely we know that we are not God. While it is certainly true that, intellectually, Christians realize they are not the creators of the universe, a look at the behavior of many tells of a different belief. Many of us suffer the stress and frustration of trying to control every facet of our lives, our world and—sometimes—even the lives of others. Returning to our definition, authentic surrender is the living out of the recognition that we are not God: recognizing and behaving in a way which acknowledges we are *not* ultimately in control of our lives, the lives of others, or of all the circumstances of our world.

This recognition does not mean we can fail to be responsible for ourselves or our world insofar as we are able to make a positive change or contribution. Surrender is not an excuse for apathy or lack of responsibility. Rather, it means that we recognize that we are not the *ultimate* power in our lives, or in the universe. As believers we must acknowledge a power greater than ourselves, not only intellectually, but in our behavior as well. We must do what we can and allow God to do the rest.

When I think about the powerful role surrender can play in our lives I am reminded of a family I have been privileged to know. The family has a young boy who had been diagnosed with bone cancer when he was just ten years old. His leg had to be amputated below the knee.

Naturally the family and the young boy suffered a lot. They dealt with fear of the cancer and of the possibility that it would spread. The boy went through the physical and emotional suffering that his situation would create for anyone. He went through the usual stages of anger and disbelief. At one point he smashed up his room in utter frustration. His mother told me she cried at the thought of him destroying his favorite things. She would have preferred he would have taken out his anger on her good china.

The young patient and his parents had long bouts of tears and depression, as you can imagine. But then, after they had vented their honest emotions and told the truth about their fears, they began to accept the fact that they could not change what had happened. Nor could they prevent such a thing from recurring. They acknowledged how grateful they were that there was no longer any sign of cancer in the boy and they began to surrender to the reality of their lives. The boy surrendered his physical self-concept and the frustration he felt at his limitations in some of the activities he loved. His parents surrendered their fears and their desire to be overprotective of their son. They surrendered their dreams of children who would not suffer and would enjoy perfect health. Together the family went through a surrender process from the clenched fists of denial, anger and a refusal to accept reality, to the open-handed position of accepting what they could not change. They became grateful for what they had and adjusted to life on the terms in which it would now necessarily be lived. This family's ability to surrender the tragedy proved to be the difference between the happy lives they now enjoy and what could have been lives spent in bitterness and obsessive fear. For them, the ability to surrender made the difference between experiencing temporary suffering, which we cannot avoid, and retreating into lives of misery, which we need not endure.

Many of us spend our lives trying not to acknowledge that we lack ultimate control of our lives. Some of us try to control our lives by controlling other people. Some of us shut ourselves off from our feelings in order to try and control the possibility of being hurt. Some people try to control life through the attainment of wealth or knowledge or success. None of these attempts to be in control work. To surrender to the reality of our lives is not to invite tragedy or practice an attitude of defeatism. Surrender, in its healthy form, means seeing the truth. Sometimes we may suffer. Other times we will celebrate. Practicing the spiritual principle of surrender means that although we set goals and try our best to achieve them and we dream dreams and give our all to making them come true, if a goal fails or a dream is broken we can begin again. After an appropriate period of time, we can stop clinging to our original expectations and learn to set new goals and dream new dreams. Living a surrendered life is not related to apathy or lethargy. It is a challenge to be ever open to new realities, new dreams, new lives and new perceptions.

In the last several years I have watched the rise of a most interesting way of avoiding surrender in the spiritual life. It has come to be called "new-age" guilt. I am referring to some of the currently popular notions such as, "A positive attitude can allow us to be in ultimate control of all of the circumstances of our lives," or "Because there are ways to control our health, we need not suffer infirmities as long as we have the right messages and practices."

I am *not* saying that a positive attitude and healthful practices are unimportant. Rather I am pointing out that these notions are flawed: We are not in complete control of our lives. When people deal with serious illness for example, some adherents of new-age guilt will attempt to figure out what the sick person did wrong to create the illness. Sometimes people become seriously ill and there just are no answers. At least not answers that our current level of science understands. Insisting that the sick person could have somehow prevented or controlled this illness is just as much a form of spiritual violence as some of the medieval horror stories about ascetics purposely damaging their own bodies for the sake of God. Sometimes there are no answers, there is only the option of surrendering in faith.

New-Age guilt results from a kind of denial that there are things in this life over which we have no control. This particular brand of guilt can lead to an "if only" trap which is lethal to the healthy spiritual life. If only I had been more positive, I would not have gotten sick. If only I had believed in my recovery from illness, I would have recovered. If only others would be different than they are, I would be happy. If only I was married instead of single, single instead of married. If only I were more thin or more wealthy or had different parents or lived in a different city. If only, if only, if only. And what we come to know is that even if all the "if onlys" come true, there will be others to take their place. Although we have an enormous amount of opportunity to make contributions to our own lives and the lives of others, in the final analysis we are not in ultimate control. Recognizing this fact is the beginning of leading the guilt-free, healthy, surrendered life.

The healthy spiritual and emotional life cannot depend on the specific circumstances of any given time because difficult circumstances are a part of life. Setting goals for ourselves, or being annoyed by other people can be a part of anyone's life. Clutching and clinging to expectations is a way of playing God and that is a sure recipe for misery.

Should we set goals and strive for them? Of course.

Should we make decisions to change our lives for the better? Without a doubt. But should we be so attached to the outcome that we are not able to be at peace unless our specific agenda is met? Only at the risk of an unhappy existence. Experiencing peace in this life necessarily includes accepting circumstances we would prefer did not exist. This lesson was pointed out to me one day by a friend of mine who is a priest.

A member of his religious community was leaving the priesthood to get married and my friend commented, "I guarantee he will not be a happily married man."

"How dare you say that about him?" I scolded. "You are just saying that because you are angry that he is leaving the community."

"That is not true," he responded. "I'm sorry if I sounded judgmental. I genuinely wish him well. It is just that I have been a priest for thirty years and I have had more than a few friends leave this community and marry. It is my observation that those men who were basically happy as priests are basically happy as married men. Those who were basically unhappy people while they were priests are basically unhappy after they leave the priesthood. I have lived with this man for ten years and the poor fellow was rarely able to accept the realities and imperfections of life—whether it was the faults and annoying habits of community members, the way the thermostat was set in the house, the food we had, the way liturgies were planned. Whatever. My comment was based on my concern that his inability to accept life's imperfections will carry over into his married life. He wasn't just unhappy in community, he was miserable about everything, every day. I just think that misery comes from within whether we live in community, the single life or married life."

Oops. Now I was the one who apologized for being judgmental. What my friend said made perfect sense. Without the ability to surrender when necessary we are sure to be miserable no matter what the details of life include. Expectations of perfection, whether of ourselves, others or the thermostat in a large old house, set us up for misery and unhappiness.

CHAPTER TWO

———————— ✦ ————————

Models of Surrender in the Bible

Surrender, remember, is living out of the recognition that we are not God. Surrender is not only an intellectual concept but an attitude which permeates our daily experiences. Surrender is not a coat we can put on and take off, but the very skin we live in. The Scriptures are full of lessons of healthy spiritual surrender. I have become convinced that, in fact, every book of the Bible is a story of surrender.

We find the temptation to play God in the very first story of the Bible. The temptation of Adam and Eve was not simply a temptation to disobey God, but a temptation to try to be something other than what they were. Remember it was the tree of knowledge and the illusion that they could be equal to God which tempted Adam and Eve. Adam and Eve were tempted to try to be God (Genesis 3:3-6). Attempting to play God can be expressed in many different ways: passing judgment, refusing to forgive, trying to control others, holding on to illusions, regret, jealousy or bitterness. Surrendering these temptations and all we are holding on to is not only an underlying theme in Genesis, it is the underlying theme in all of Scripture. From the first page to the last, the Scriptures invite and challenge us to let go of all that we clutch on to, and to release our clenched fists of control, transforming them into the open hands of acceptance.

Each book of the Bible includes accounts of people who struggle with letting go of the things to which they cling. Abraham was called to surrender what he loved most, his son Isaac (Genesis 22: 1-14), and to trust even when the call of God did not seem to make sense. Although Abraham knew that following God's request to sacrifice his son would cause him great pain, he kept his part of the covenant he made with God. He would acknowledge God as God and accept his role as a child of God. Abraham had to be willing to surrender his own dreams, ideas, pleasures and plans. The story of God's request and Abraham's subsequent surrender to God is a difficult one but one that is central to confirming the covenant between God and humankind. Ongoing theological arguments regarding the historicity of the story and details of the covenant certainly seem to be of secondary importance to the very clear message that the God of the Bible is a higher power than any of us individually and that the recognition of that reality is a sacred thing.

In the story of Exodus we see the journey of the Israelites crossing the desert which mirrors our own journeys across the deserts of our lives. As with the Israelites, we often pull back in fear when confronted with difficult times. And, as with the Israelites, we are called to surrender that fear and trust in God. It is particularly important to remember the covenant God made with the people of Israel. In its most basic form, it is a statement regarding spiritual surrender: God will be God and the people (the Israelites) will be God's people. Although there are many theological interpretations of this story and the concept of God's chosen people, the reality that God is God and those who seek to follow are asked to trust God and not compete with God is clear. Those who enter into the covenant enter into a sacred agreement to allow God to be the God of their lives and to accept the reality of who they are as human beings—sacred beings, granted, but human nonetheless.

The story of Job offers us another scriptural example regarding our relationship with God. From the Book of Job we discover we are called not only to surrender the distressing losses of our lives but ultimately to even surrender the desire to know the "why" of our circumstances (Job 37, 42). Job received more than he ever hoped for or longed for after he recognized that he was not God and would not know all of the reasons behind the circumstances of his life. Thus Job attained all he needed and more.

The New Testament begins with the story of Mary's surrender to the will of God regardless of the burdens she might face in carrying out God's will. When confronted with the announcement that, though a virgin, she would conceive and bear a child, Mary quite possibly faced the loss of her fiancé, the disrespect of her community, the disappointment of her parents, misjudgment and (according to the religious laws of her time) possibly even death. Still, believing that the request was truly from God, Mary boldly surrendered to it saying, "Behold I am the handmaid of the Lord; let it be done to me according to your will" (Luke 1:38). For Christians, Mary's surrender offers a perfect model of open hands. Mary's surrender also ushers in the age of the messiah and makes an important statement about the role of surrender: First we are called to surrender to God. Then salvation is possible.

From Mary's profound example to the disciples who are called to leave their homes, occupations and all that is familiar, we are given stories of people who are called to surrender. Peter is asked to surrender his judgment of Matthew. Religious leaders are called to surrender their self-righteousness and the rigidity of their laws and theology. Repeatedly, people are asked to surrender their fears, their grudges and the ethnic, political, social and religious prejudices of a lifetime. Then in the ultimate story of surrender, Jesus, though full of anxiety and fear, offers his own life if it be the will of his Father (Matthew 26:42).

Page after page, chapter after chapter, the Scriptures share with us stories of surrender and the primary place surrender holds in the spiritual life. And we are assured by the resurrection of Jesus that we will not be left in the lonely and dark cave of letting go. Our surrender to God's will and God's ways will most surely lead to resurrections in our own lives. This is the message of each story of the Bible. Though many times we cry out to God to take the cup of suffering from us, in the final analysis we are called to surrender to the way of God.

But how do we know what is the will of God? Surely the suffering we see all around us cannot be the will of God. Does surrender mean apathy in the face of injustice? Is surrender a crutch, the result of weakness of character? Haven't we been raised to admire the one who never gives up?

Religious people have struggled for centuries to understand the concept of surrender in the spiritual life. As we look back over history we find leaders asking people to deny their honest feelings or talents in the name of religious surrender. We find whole nations being asked to give up their heritage, their language, their culture, even their sacred concepts of God in surrendering to another culture and religion. There are numerous cases of emotional and psychological harm done to individuals by others who believed they were following—often through the guidance of a religious leader of some sort—the dictate to surrender everything to God. At times, the concept of surrender has been interpreted in less than godly ways. Perhaps this is why surrender has fallen out of focus in some Christian circles.

Recent years have witnessed an outcry from critics of twelve-step self-help groups. Twelve-step groups emphasize surrendering one's life to a higher power. Some therapists claim that letting go of control in one's life and surrendering to a higher power creates a permanent self-concept of helplessness and victimization. Some individuals who have been harmed by misguided ideas of spiritual surrender feel an understandable hesitation. The issue can be confusing. Just how does one discern godly surrender from misconceptions that are harmful?

Using Jesus as a model, it can be seen that authentic spiritual surrender always comes from a position of strength, honesty and emotional health. If the surrender comes out of weakness, illusion or fear, then it is not authentic. It is not the product of free choice. In order to offer an authentic free gift, one must be free of coercion and force. Force would cancel out the merit of the gift. Had Jesus been forced to say, "Father forgive them, they know not what they do" (Luke 23:34), his forgiveness would have been meaningless. Personal freedom is the hallmark of one who drops his or her illusions and with strength of character can say, "I surrender to the things I cannot change."

The spiritual masters of the Bible were not perfect people. They were flawed. But when they surrendered to God it was with their eyes wide open. They were in a state of personal (if not always physical) freedom. The authentic spiritual surrender modeled by so many in the Scriptures was not related to apathy or illusion or fear. It was real and came from awareness and strength; it always came from truth and love. That is what made the surrender holy.

In the following chapters we will look at ways to become aware, to experience the truth and love that will assure us that our surrender is godly, and not misguided.

CHAPTER THREE

The Steps to Surrender

Step One: Identifying the Truth

Healthy religious surrender is always based on the truth, free of illusion. It is important to note that it is not necessarily our hopes or desires which destroy our surrender but the way we continue to cling to them when they have not been realized. Remember, Jesus let his desire or preference be known to the Father when he said, "If it is possible for this cup to pass from me, let it," but after having made his desire known, he surrendered all clinging to that desire by saying, "Not my will, but your will be done" (Luke 22:41).

Similarly we may desire, for example, to have perfect health. Preferring health over illness is certainly not unholy. Yet clutching onto our health in a controlling and demanding way as in, "I will not be happy or peaceful if I do not enjoy perfect health!" is an example of blocking the spiritual principle of surrender. Further, once we have done all we can to ensure good health, if we find ourselves seriously ill, surrender means accepting the situation and responding to it in emotionally, psychologically and spiritually mature ways. My grandmother used to put it this way, "Accept the cards you have been dealt and continue your participation in the game. If one hand of cards puts you out of the game, gear up for the next game which will be coming along shortly."

Identifying the truth can also be thought of as facing the reality of a given situation. We will talk more specifically about how to learn to distinguish the truth from illusion in Chapter Five. For now it is important to stress the foundational role that searching for the truth plays in our search for surrender.

When we hold onto fantasies of how we *want* things to be, we move away from the truth and closer to misery. For example, if a person confronted with poor health holds on to bitterness, that would only be a recipe for misery. It is an example of the frustration which results from playing God. (As God, we would ordain perfect health for ourselves.) Accepting another reality means accepting the fact that we are not and cannot be in ultimate control of our lives and world; we cannot be God. That is the first and most important truth we must identify.

Still, accepting that we do not have ultimate power over our health does not relieve us of the significant influence we do have. Refusing to exercise and eating foods you know to be harmful while stating, "I have surrendered my health to God," has nothing to do with surrender.

In order to identify the truth of a given situation, there are a number of steps we can take. First, we must be open to the possibility that we may be wrong. That's right: Our presumptions, attitudes and opinions may be wrong. Being open to changing our perceptions can be one of the most difficult steps on the road to surrender. We have all been conditioned in a number of ways to see things in a particular way. Our personal experiences, ethnic and national enculturation, religious training and education have all conditioned us. In order to be open to reassessing our views and attitudes, we have to let go of this conditioning. In some areas our conditioning may help us to be open-minded and objective, but in others it might fill us with misperceptions attached to inappropriate emotional responses.

Another key to identifying the truth is to seek the advice of others. To be sure that the advice is unbiased, it is a good idea to seek out a professional counselor or spiritual mentor. Tell your story to someone else. Ask them to tell you how it sounds to them. Be brave enough to hear the response without blaming them. If you are uncomfortable with what you hear, do not hesitate to ask another person. Keep asking until a sense of reality begins to become clear. Notice any themes that consistently appear in the way others hear your story.

A woman once told me a story about how her twenty-seven-year-old son had abandoned her by getting married and moving to a city several hours away. She was outraged. She was miserable. She blamed her new daughter-in-law for "turning her son against her." She was in real pain; she felt abandoned and unloved by her son. However, as I heard her story, I wondered if the real source of her pain was something else in her background—perhaps some kind of abandonment that occurred before her son was even born. I acknowledged that I do not have a son, but it seemed healthy and normal to me to have an adult child get married and move away from home where employment opportunities were more abundant.

She was not very receptive to my point of view. In fact she became angry with me and called me insensitive. And then she made a most important declaration. She stated that my response had been just as insensitive as those of her friends, her pastor and her two sisters.

If we are brave enough to seek the honest opinions of others about our struggles and we are repeatedly met with the same general responses, it is our responsibility to at least consider the *possibility* that the messages we are receiving may contain important insights that we should not ignore.

The difficult aspect of that woman's pain was that her feelings of abandonment were so strong she was drowning in them and was unable to hear the many consistent messages that were given to her. If you find yourself in a similar situation while searching for the truth, do not hesitate to seek the help of a professional counselor who may be able to help you uncover the layers of emotional pain or confusion that are blocking your progress toward surrender.

A third key to identifying the truth we seek in our journey toward surrender is to remember that this truth will be free of the unhealed wounds of the past. Unhealed pain can distort the truth. The truth that sets us free becomes clearer to us as we heal past wounds.

For example, a woman who has deeply hurt your feelings may have left you the understandable impression that she is without compassion. Although *your* experience of her may have been compassionless, a search for the objective truth may well reveal a very complex person who is driven more by fear than by desires to hurt. It would be much easier to truly see the person who hurt your feelings if you work on healing the hurt she caused before you make such a judgment.

The truth we seek is free of the habit of projecting past hurts onto others. For example, if you had a critical father who hurt you repeatedly with cruel comments about your ineptness, you must be careful not to unleash that pent-up anger on a boss or teacher who offers constructive criticism. Such confused reactions happen so often in our society that we can almost hear a plea to find the objective truth. Uncover it and deal with it on its own terms. Identify the pain your father inflicted upon you and work on healing it and placing it in an appropriate perspective. Identify the criticism from your boss or teacher for exactly what it is. Analyze the comments on their own merits, free from the pain of past criticism. If you are able to do this you have begun to identify and live in the truth.

Step Two: Letting Go of Illusion

It is not always easy to know if our perceptions and emotions are based on the truth. Yet authentic, healthy surrender is always related to a clear-sighted understanding of the truth. We cannot surrender something if we do not know we are holding on to it. This fact is often forgotten while people struggle fruitlessly in an attempt to surrender a situation they do not fully understand. That is why it is often necessary to seek outside perspectives regarding the identification of the truth in a given situation.

The next step in the process of surrender requires us to acknowledge that we may not know or understand everything that contributes to our struggle with surrender. We must take some time in realizing that we are not God and that there is indeed a divine power that can help us.

As we discussed earlier, we first acknowledge that we are not God, then we identify the truth of a situation as clearly as we are able. Surrender is the result of facing reality. This can be painful. Often, in an attempt to avoid that pain, people opt for drowning in illusion. Choosing that option brings even more pain, though it provides short-term relief. Such a choice can only prolong our misery because it simply covers the truth in illusory icing. In order to be emotionally, psychologically and spiritually free, we have no option but to find the truth of ourselves, others and our life. The more illusion in our lives, the more we are forced to cling to it in order to protect that illusion. The more illusion in our lives, the more we have layers keeping us from facing the truth, which we must do for surrender to take place.

If, for example, a man finds it impossible to surrender a lost love after a reasonable period of time, he obsesses and frets about losing the only true love of his life, and he fails to function effectively in his life. Simply advising him to surrender the pain and loss to God is sure to be met with failure, if not outright hostility.

In uncovering the truth of that situation, understanding

the difference between love and dependency, his concept of self, the illusion of the concept of "one true love," could all surface. It is likely that what he needs to surrender has more to do with his own self-concept, dependency issues or illusions about the object of his obsession than it has to do with "the loss of his one great love." Surrender cannot take place unless it is based on the objective truth. After struggling to surrender a loss for a reasonable period of time it would be important for such a man to ask why it is so difficult to surrender this particular issue. (The definition of a "reasonable" period of time is ultimately determined by each individual. When we are truly ready, we will surrender. Anthony DeMello put it another way when he said, "When we are sick of being miserable, we will wake up." Although friends and family can give us clues that it may be time to reassess our understanding of "reasonable," we cannot authentically surrender because someone else wants us to.) A serious exploration of the "why" may result in answers such as, "Because I'm afraid no one else will love me." Now we can begin to see that what is being clutched on to is not just one relationship, but a deep-seated insecurity as well. Unless the insecurities are addressed, authentic surrender of the loss will never take place.

Let's look at one of our earlier examples in more detail. It will help us to see how a lack of awareness and illusion interferes with the ability to authentically surrender. Suppose a college student unconsciously carried with them the voice of an extremely critical parent. The parent's constant insults, put-downs and criticism of her has left her insecure and oversensitive to criticism. Now, although away at college, and living quite a distance from her parents, she confronts a situation which seems to be new and specific, but is actually rooted in the criticism she received in the past. If her professor corrected her term paper with numerous suggestions for improvement she may assume, based on voices of the past, that the professor thinks her incapable of college-level work, or doesn't like her personally, or perhaps even has some kind of grudge against her. She might tell a friend of her anger toward the professor. If her friend suggests that she simply surrender her anger, it is unlikely she could follow that suggestion, even if she wanted to. In order to understand her current situation, she would have to first understand how this experience has been colored by having had a critical parent. Only then could she effectively begin the process to authentic surrender.

Some years ago I was working as a pastoral minister and teaching theology at a university. Through a complex series of events and much to my surprise, I found myself in a social setting one evening with a group of drug smugglers. They spent some time bragging about the large sums of money they enjoyed due to outsmarting the Drug Enforcement Agency. Then they asked me, "What do you do for a living?"

When I answered, they laughed and said, "No really, what do you do?"

After finally convincing them that I truly was a minister in a Catholic Church and a theology teacher, the conversation took a most surprising turn.

One young man suddenly volunteered that he "used to be a Catholic" and told me the following story: When he was a child preparing for his First Communion, his grandmother gave him an empty baby food jar and a handful of kernels of corn. She told him that in order to know that he was really making an effort to be worthy of the sacrament he should "make sacrifices." Every time he made his brother's bed or helped with the dishes without being asked, he could put a kernel of corn in the jar. When the jar was full, according to his grandmother, he would be ready to receive his First Communion.

To my utter amazement, this young man who had been bragging about vile crimes not ten minutes before suddenly threw his shoulders back with pride, smiled and said, "You know, I filled up that whole jar!" Our conversation continued as the others joined in with their own stories and the "lapsed Catholic" related how he began to "get into trouble," how it hurt his mother, and how he often thought of that baby food jar to remind himself that "he was not all bad." As my original plans for the evening were clearly not going to materialize and I was left without transportation, I asked my newfound friends if they would drive me to a nearby restaurant where my car was parked. They agreed and continued their stories as we drove. It was there that my troubles with surrender began.

The impromptu religious-discussion-group members drove me to the restaurant in their rented limousine. Each one got out of the car with me to say good-bye and to make sure I found my way safely to my car. There I stood in the parking lot with four heavily bejeweled men, who were dressed in particularly unsubtle apparel, standing next to a white stretch limo, when I saw one of my students through the window of the restaurant. She looked horrified. I actually saw her mouth the words, "Oh my God, it's my theology teacher!"

If surrender can be symbolized by open, outstretched hands, at that moment my hands clutched into tight fists of panic. What must she think of me? How would she ever understand? And this was not just any student but one who often came by my office to tell me of her spiritual struggles or important issues in her life. She told me that I was the only theology teacher with whom she felt comfortable being honest about her religious opinions. It is a lesson in humility to look back at that now and realize that I took in her comments with pleasure thinking that I must be really swell.

Now I was faced with her confusion and disappointment and a professional dilemma. She was a student, after all, and not a personal friend. I did not owe her an explanation, yet I did not want her to misunderstand. It was difficult to experience her changed attitude toward me at school. I wondered if she discussed what she saw with other students. I nearly drove the staff of the parish where I worked crazy from my constant fretting about the incident. Day after day I worried about what my student might think and how I should handle the situation. Finally one afternoon the pastor came to my office and told me he had been thinking about the situation. I looked at him eagerly, hoping he had some solution which would allow me to regain the admiration of my student and put an end to her confusion. This is what he said: "She has a savior and you are not it!"

That afternoon brought quite a lesson both in humility and in surrender. When considering the pastor's words I had to admit that I most certainly was not my student's savior. I had no control over how she chose to interpret what she saw. I had no control over whether she shared her interpretation. And the most difficult thing of all was admitting that the majority of my concern was for my own reputation—not for my student. I meditated and prayed to be able to surrender the whole incident, keep my mind on being loving and to walk with what my pastor called "silent integrity."

How fortunate I was to work with a truly wise man. As he left he said, "Sometimes people will never understand no matter how hard we try to make them. Letting go is the only sane and godly thing to do. You cannot control this situation. Peace will come when you realize and accept that."

Step Three: Dealing With the Truth We Have Discovered

Finding the truth is not easy. And, once found, it can be painful to embrace. It is hard to look at ourselves truthfully and admit selfishness or a lack of integrity in our lives or self-concept. Without simple honesty, however, authentic surrender cannot take place. In the process of surrender we must start at the truth—or as close as we are able to get to it—and be open to new interpretations of ourselves or anyone or anything else. Surrender can be a difficult and time-consuming process, but it is the bridge between the frustrated life of someone trying vainly to be always in control and the peaceful life of someone who has learned to accept what cannot be changed.

There are many parts of the spiritual journey which

must be walked alone but there are other times when the journey requires a companion. If we think of the spiritual journey to surrender as a trip up a beautiful mountain we will realize the need for companions. Though the mountain is indeed beautiful and once we reach a plateau close enough to the top we can take in the breathtaking view and rest in a peaceful state, it is also full of rough terrain. There are rocks to trip over and dangerous footholds. It only makes sense to take companions along for the journey. When we need help climbing a difficult cliff our companions can assist us. We can do the same for them when they are in need of encouragement.

Our spiritual companions can be friends, church groups, neighbors, professional spiritual mentors, psychologists, psychiatrists or family members. Each will have different insights to offer and different skills to help on the journey up that mountain. Do not be afraid to ask for help. And, do not be afraid of someone telling you they are not in a position to go on the journey with you right now. That bit of honesty is much more helpful than having a resistant or disgruntled companion!

Once we have dropped our illusions and discovered the truth to the best of our ability, we are ready to continue following the steps to surrender. In the following chapters we will continue our look at the steps to surrender by examining unhealthy concepts of surrender and the role self-awareness plays.

Unhealthy Concepts of Surrender

Like any concept, surrender can be manipulated into an unhealthy form. Working toward our own health should never include violence, manipulation, coercion or fear. By learning to surrender, we let go of all attempts to be controlling: We do what we can the best we can, and leave the rest to God. This can become unhealthy when we surrender to other people, material things or our own fears.

Surrender is not healthy if it is forced by religious laws

rather than freely offered from the heart. Surrender must come from *you*. No one—not even the Church or your spiritual guides—can surrender for you, especially if they try to do so through commands, threats or rules.

Surrender is not healthy if it is based on fear. Some examples of this would be:

"I'm afraid you will leave me if I go back to school so I will surrender my desire for an education."

"If I am angry I will be behaving in an un-Christian way. I will be a bad person if I am angry. I am afraid of being considered a bad person so I will not acknowledge my anger, even to myself."

Surrender is not healthy if it causes emotional violence (or any kind of violence). Any denial of your true feelings is emotional violence. If you are deeply hurt but pretend you are not because you think expressing it would be selfish or "unholy," consider the value of healthy emotional behavior. Pretense is certainly not holy, and if you are not careful it can quickly grow into serious neurosis. If you have been hurt, one of the first steps to surrender is simply to acknowledge that you have been hurt. Telling yourself that you should not be hurt or that you should hurry and get over it will only make you feel worse and prolong the surrender process. Once you acknowledge the truth of your feelings, you can decide how to act upon them.

CHAPTER FOUR

---❀---

Surrender and Self-Awareness

The Target of Awareness

One of the most important ingredients in surrender is self-awareness. As we have said before, it is impossible to surrender something that you are not aware of. Often what we try to surrender has roots from years past. Trying to surrender hurt feelings related to a friend's comment is, of course, important, but if the hurt is rooted in a childhood spent with a severely critical parent (to revisit our previous example), those childhood experiences must be addressed along with your reaction to your friend's comment.

Self-awareness—seeing the truth about ourselves, free of illusion—is essential for a happy productive life. Developing self-awareness is a lifelong process. But there are ways to increase your self-awareness immediately. Consider what I call the "target of awareness." Imagine the image on the next page as a target:

Illustration of Target of Awareness

LAYERS OF
ENCULTURATION

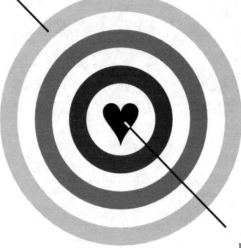

PERSONAL
FREEDOM

Most people live on the outermost edges of self-awareness, remaining puppets of their childhood and cultural conditioning. At the center of the target is our truest self. There we are free of false images of ourselves and others, free of false expectations. In the center of the target we are personally free. We are keenly aware of those things that have strongly influenced us in both positive and negative ways. From our center we see ourselves realistically. We recognize where we need emotional or spiritual healing, and begin that healing. We recognize and celebrate our special talents—false humility has no place here. We recognize the hard work that has helped us achieve our goals and are grateful for what we have accomplished. We do not brag over our achievements, and we do not berate ourselves for our failures. This center of personal freedom is a source of peace and contentment.

The further we get from our center, the less aware we are, and the more we tend to react according to our conditioning rather than our true selves. Away from our center, surrender becomes more difficult—and more necessary. Most of us must travel through many layers of conditioning and self-deception to find our center.

The layers of the target represent our experiences and influences: all of the messages we have been given about ourselves, others or life. Some of us understand what those layers are—which experiences have affected us most deeply, which influences still have a powerful effect. Others may not be aware of how profoundly our conditioning shapes us. They do not understand why they are always angry, or self-critical or envious. Some are so devastated when one of their illusions is destroyed that they hold on to the loss, filling their lives with the misery of a single mistake or a single misunderstanding.

We are responsible for the damage such a lack of self-awareness can cause if we do nothing to prevent it. And this damage does not stop at our own bodies and lives—it can harm others as well. Perhaps you know of a parent who targets one of his children when venting disappointment or anger (perhaps you are that parent, or were that child). Studies show that a large number of such parents choose the child they think is most like themselves. So, unconsciously, the parent transfers his own self-hatred to the child that most reminds him of himself, creating pain for both.

Most of us have some sort of "normal" neurosis—fears, judgmentalism, moments of meanness or depression. A lack of self-awareness, for us "normal neurotics," truly seems to be the root of all evil. Certainly it is the root of most harmful, or sinful, behavior. Trying to understand who we are and why we behave the way we do is the first step to healing the causes of our sinful behavior, allowing us to behave differently in the future. (Please note, though, that our definitions here are not appropriate to someone with a serious mental illness, such as a sociopath or a violent psychopath.)

With each insight, we are a step closer to living from the center of our target and being our truest, most peaceful, selves.

Modes of Thought

One of the most important ways to begin to grow in awareness is to understand our most commonly used modes of thought. Modes of thought are, basically, the thinking habits that we have developed. They represent the way we tend to perceive our world. Our thinking can be a knee-jerk reaction based on our conditioning or carefully considered—ideas which are the result of awareness and the practice of surrender.

Consider the following modes of thought. Which one do you use most often? Understanding these modes can serve as a measure of your level of self-awareness, as well as a guide to the kind of thinker you want to be.

The Reactionary Mode. The reactionary mode is an emotional reaction based on conditioning. For example, if you are asked about a controversial issue—such as capital punishment—and you immediately respond emotionally and with fierce judgment, regardless of the side you take, you are responding with your feelings, not your thoughts.

There is nothing wrong with being passionate about your opinion, as long as it is *your* opinion. But how many of us simply adopt the position of our parents, teachers or friends without really thinking through the issue? And, even of those few who do take the time to become well-informed on an issue, how many of us have been able to escape our conditioning and break through to understand what *we* really believe?

We will discuss conditioning in the next sections, but it is important to realize the difference between those things we have a conditioned response to and those things we have considered objectively.

I once taught at a college that advertised itself with the

slogan: "It's not what you think, but how you think." I loved that ad. It works not only in reference to educated, informed opinions, but self-awareness as well.

In order to teach my students the difference between the reactionary mode and an objective thought, I ask them to choose a controversial topic, one with distinct pro and con positions, and the position for which they would like to argue. After collecting their papers, I would have them write a term paper on the topic they had chosen, argued from the position *opposite* their own. I explained that an opinion is only as significant as the effort made to form it from the facts. It is essential to look at all sides of an issue before drawing a conclusion. Examining some of our most closely held opinions can be an eye-opening adventure in self-awareness.

Do you know why you hold the opinions you do? Do you know why certain things set you off emotionally and others do not? Have you truly formed your opinions, or have you let them form you?

During the last presidential campaign I overheard a group of third- and fourth-graders arguing for the candidate of their "choice." They shouted back and forth "yea" for one or "boo" for the other. On and on they argued as I stood amazed at the strong conditioning of those children. Is it possible that some of them formed their opinions from a careful consideration of the issues facing the nation? It is more likely, of course, that they were simply imitating their parents. The whole scene of grade-schoolers was endearing, but for adults such reactionary responses are problematic, even dangerous. Some people—maybe even most—vote from their conditioning. Some marry, choose jobs, raise children and pass on religious views in the same way, rather than using the intellect God has given them to form knowledgeable opinions. Of course, you may carefully examine an issue and wind up drawing the same conclusion your parents did. That's fine. But thinking through an issue means that even if you wind up right back at what your grandmother told you, now you know that it is also truly your conclusion as well.

The Reflective Mode. The reflective mode of thought is based upon your honest reflections on a topic; it includes a recognition of the limits of your background on the issue. Let's use our example of capital punishment. If you are asked your opinion and you know you have not carefully studied the issue, you can certainly talk about what you do know, while acknowledging there is more you could learn about it. This is a key aspect of self-awareness: knowing what you do not know.

Simply take time to reflect upon what you do know, think or feel. Consider how you developed your feelings or opinions—it is a wonderful way to grow in self-awareness. Keeping a journal is one way to work through your reflections; talking with a trusted friend is another. Having a spiritual director, making a retreat, participating in therapy or a twelve-step group are other ways of getting to know yourself and becoming more self-aware. But always be honest enough to admit (to yourself and others) the limits of your knowledge or understanding. Reflecting upon your relationship with your sister, for example, would be an excellent exercise in self-awareness; but your sister may not remember the same things you do, or she may remember them differently. So reflecting alone may not be enough to help you fully understand your sister or similar family issues. It can be difficult to acknowledge our human limits, but that is part of the very definition of surrender. After all, we are not God.

Obviously we cannot all be experts in everything. It is unreasonable to think that we can be fully informed about every issue. But, we can make sure that our opinions and behaviors are not based simply on our conditioning. Instead of discussing our half-explored thoughts on a subject, we can spend that time developing a deeper understanding of both ourselves and the issue at hand. And rather than defending our unreflective opinions, we can be open to new information that others can provide. The next time someone has an opinion different from your own, listen carefully to what they have to say and consider—honestly—that they may be right. This will help you develop the conclusion that is truly right for you.

The Critical Mode. Ideally critical thought involves research. Back to our example of capital punishment, most people have never carefully studied it, but most have strong opinions about it. Even if your ideas about capital punishment are based on other values—you may believe that it is never right to take the life of another—it is always important to look at an issue critically before forming a conclusion. You may not change your conclusion but your conclusion will be more informed and you will be better able to discuss your ideas.

Critical thought involves being precise in your definitions, asking questions, looking at every side of the issue, listening to the views of others and then drawing a conclusion. To critically analyze the topic of capital punishment we would first define the term and read and study as much as possible about the topic. What exactly do you mean when you talk about capital punishment? What is the goal of capital punishment? What do the statistics show about its effectiveness based on the goals it is supposed to achieve? What does your religious tradition say about it? What do informed people on both sides of this issue say in their arguments? Do the Scriptures discuss it specifically? If not, do the Scriptures say something about a related topic?

After approaching the topic as objectively and openmindedly as possible, and adding the specific information available to you, draw a conclusion—still remaining open to new information which may come your way. We are purposely using an emotionally charged topic here as an example to give us a chance to consider how open we really are to the wisdom life has to teach us. Simply saying "I know I am right" is not using critical thought. In the spiritual life—and especially in the practice of surrender—it is never appropriate to close off our minds to any ideas. Even when some conclusions seem obvious, being open-minded is in itself a healthy spiritual practice.

Critical thought is what we want from jurors and judges. It is objective, not based on emotion or prejudice. It is the result of open-mindedness and careful analysis. At its best, critical thought involves wisdom, the kind of thought and knowledge the Bible esteems and teaches. In fact the sacred writings of every major world religion instruct people to grow in wisdom. Wisdom is the knowledge that comes from God. Closed-mindedness or intellectual arrogance is never spiritually healthy. Whatever we know about ourselves or any topic, acknowledging that there is always more God may want to teach us, is a spiritual attitude which leads to surrender, and through surrender to wisdom.

Every time I think about spiritual arrogance I am reminded of an experience I had while I was working as a parish minister. A member of our parish, a young mother of three little boys had an inherited disease and was going blind. I went to visit her one day and found her struggling to handle her homemaking tasks. Her boys were energetically running amok in the house—perhaps unconsciously taking advantage of their mother's inability to see what they were up to. When we talked about the progression of her illness, she said that she was not worried. She was making a novena to Saint Therese, the Little Flower, and she was sure she would get the miracle for which she hoped. (The tradition involves saying a prayer to Saint Therese every day for nine days asking her to intercede for you before the Lord. On the ninth day, if your petition has been granted you will receive a rose, one of the symbols of Saint Therese. As part of the novena, you should not tell anyone you are saying it—to keep others from sending the rose to console you.)

I was overwhelmed with sadness at the suffering of this young woman and her family, but I said nothing when she mentioned the novena. Frankly, I was caught off-guard. But as I thought about her situation, I was filled with a kind of frustration. I thought: What this woman needs is some counseling to help her deal with the reality of her situation, and some help to take care of these boys. She certainly does not need to be making novenas to Saint Therese. In ten years of theological study I had never heard anyone talk seriously about novenas, except to list them in the category of popular piety. Novenas were not based on Scripture or solid contemporary theological thought. I left her house feeling sad, frustrated and intellectually arrogant. "Novenas to Saint Therese," I thought to myself, "What a waste of time! Imagine such a thing!" I made a mental note to speak to the pastor about getting this woman some *real* help.

Still upset from my visit, I went to a friend's house for lunch. This friend is a theologically educated, highly intelligent and practical woman. She had just experienced what must be one of a mother's worst nightmares. One of her children—a lovely, kind teenage daughter—had been brutally assaulted by a stranger. This family is one of the finest examples of family I have ever known. The parents are loving and involved in their children's lives. They are active members of their parish, always ready to help anyone. They are extremely generous with their time and money whenever they hear of a need. The news of the assault horrified everyone—first for the usual reasons, but also, I believe, because this girl and her family were so uncommonly good. They did everything right. They were completely dedicated to their family, their friends and God. Even the most adamant victim-blamer could not find a way to make this tragedy this family's fault in any way. Being good did not keep evil out of their lives. Taking precautions, being sensible, having a positive outlook, loving God...none of these things prevented evil from touching the lives of these good people.

As we had lunch, I began to tell my friend about the experience I had just had and how upset I was to think of that young mother saying novenas to Saint Therese.

"Isn't it just horrible that she is saying novenas instead of going to counseling?" I sighed. My friend said nothing.

"Don't you think it is just silly and sad?" I pressed on. Still I got no response. Her silence was unusual and it was clear something was up. "What are you thinking?" I asked her. "Why aren't you saying anything?"

My friend invited me upstairs to her room. Over the bed was a painting of a single red rose. She told me that when her family was in the worst of their suffering she longed for the days when life seemed so much safer—the days when she literally had the faith of a child. She had always loved Saint Therese and when she felt overwhelmed from the tragedy she found her novena card to Saint Therese and prayed, "Just let me know I have the strength to get through this and be what I need to be for my daughter and the rest of the family."

In keeping with the tradition, my friend told no one about her novena. On the ninth day, her daughter—the one who had been so hurt—came home from school and asked if they could have a talk. As they sat down to talk she thanked her mother for being there for her in such a loving and strong way. She also thanked her for bearing the brunt of her anger: "I'm sorry if I lashed out at you, Mom. I guess I knew that you would love me anyway, but it doesn't seem fair to you. I don't know what I would do without you. I love you so much Mom. Thank you, thank you, for being so strong and dependable."

Mother and daughter were both in tears. Almost as an afterthought the younger woman pulled something from her schoolbag and said, "Oh yeah. I made this for you in art class today." It was the painting of the one red rose.

Now I was in tears. My friend simply stated that she would appreciate it if I would not make fun of Saint Therese or novenas! "Sometimes," she said to me, "you are just not interested in what theologians have to say. You need the faith tradition you were given as a child. You need the comfort, the simplicity and, for me, the confidence you gain from it. This was not a time when I wanted to discuss Christology or Vatican II politics. I just needed to know I would have the strength to be able to give my family what they needed for as long as they needed it. Saint Therese was a young woman who suffered much and my daughter was suffering. I thought of Saint Therese, I prayed to her, and through her God answered me in an overwhelmingly beautiful way."

I learned a powerful lesson that day. As I drove home I found myself wondering about things like novenas and people who do receive those roses. I wondered if Carl Jung's concept of the collective unconscious could have been at work or the powerful psychic connection between mother and child could have put the idea of the rose in the daughter's mind. Then I remembered my friend's words and laughed at myself. What did it matter what theologians or psychologists said? At that painful moment in her life, my friend had surrendered so much: She did not blame God for the incident; she did not spend the rest of her life obsessing over the unanswerable why's; she did not resent those whose families have been spared such suffering. She knew what she needed—confidence in her strength to deal with her situation. She asked, and her prayer was answered. Some would consider her decision to make a novena superstitious, or at least, a product of noncritical thought. But since true critical thought always includes being open-minded, I realized that I was the one guilty of noncritical thought: I had been intellectually arrogant. I vowed I would never be so quick to judge another's way of approaching God again.

Reflecting on this incident, I was struck with yet another lesson. If either of the two women I had visited that day had been Hindu or Buddhist, I would never have judged their rituals or approach to God. I was shocked to realize how quick I was to judge people from my own tradition when I would have been genuinely respectful of someone else's religious tradition. Arrogance and conditioning, including, I realized, my own academic conditioning, can be a lethal combination. Novenas may not be my favorite way to approach God but when I realized how quick I was to judge something so personal and sacred as someone else's chosen form of prayer (especially because they were Catholic like me and I somehow felt I had the right!), I felt I had had a lesson in critical thought I would never forget. And I haven't.

Sometime later I again visited the young mother who was going blind. Her eyesight was worse. I asked her if she felt betrayed by Saint Therese because she did not receive a rose and her petition was not being granted. "Oh no," she said emphatically, "I love Saint Therese. I guess I have to face that this is the life God has chosen for me. Anyway I know Saint Therese understands. She suffered a lot of physical pain in her life, you know, and she was only a young girl. It is always good to know there are those who understand, especially someone so close to God, you know?" Yes, I did know. I told her that I admired her choosing her own path and timetable to come to terms with the direction her life was taking. She seemed astonished at my comment and said, "But that's not a really big deal, is it?" Yes, I told her, I thought it was a very big deal.

I have often thought of these two women and how each enriched my own journey to surrender in countless ways. I am grateful to have had both of them as gifts in my life. One I knew for a short time and the other remains a treasured friend. They both reminded me in powerful ways that one of the foundational elements of spiritual maturity is being open-minded. Each step we take in learning to surrender and to grow in self-awareness is a step closer to finding our way home to the center of ourselves and to God.

Being aware of the kinds of thought modes we tend most to employ is a sure help in the path to greater self-awareness. Later, we will talk about specific exercises that you can do to improve your self-awareness on a daily basis.

CHAPTER FIVE

---❈---

Enculturation

Another key to understanding ourselves and our progress toward the target of self-awareness is enculturation. Enculturation, for our purposes, is the sum total of influences in our lives. All of the events, circumstances and experiences of our lives can condition our perspective. If we fail to understand the extent of that conditioning, we cannot hope to work through it to a more honest, fact-based view of the world. The more we are conscious of our enculturation and its specific impact on our behavior and attitudes, the closer we move to the center of our target of self-awareness.

Of course, we cannot change past events that have influenced us, but we can recognize their influence and begin to heal what needs to be healed. We can discover, own and herald the objective truth about ourselves. If we find we still have bitterness from childhood experiences or divorces—all right, we are one step closer to self-awareness.

The next step is to find ways to heal the emotional wounds. Growing in self-awareness helps us accept the faults, failings and even the emotional sickness of others. At the same time, it can also free us of the bonds of trying to live up to (or down to) someone else's expectations. We become free to know who we are at our center and to shout from the mountaintops: I am clever! I am compassionate! I am talented! By recognizing these things from the personal freedom of our center, we loose the chains of unhealthy conditioning which told us that knowing the positive truth about ourselves was prideful. It is sad to consider how far some of us have traveled away from graciously acknowledging the gifts God has given us and simply being joyful about them.

Growing in self-awareness can be painful as we uncover some of the hidden wounds in our lives or the illusions we have long held. But the process of going through the layers of our enculturation, and walking through them layer by layer toward our center is sure to be worth the price. At the same time it also brings with it tremendous unburdening as we joyfully claim, "I can do what I have longed to do!" or "I am a sacred person worthy of success and happiness in my life!" These are not simple affirmations. This is a realization—we *know* the truth about ourselves. We are not trying to talk ourselves into believing "I'm OK." We *know* we are OK and have security in the truth we have found. Authentic surrender teaches us to acknowledge our goodness and potential as well as our pains and difficulties. False humility and a self-deprecating attitude are not part of healthy surrender. Seeking the truth so that it can indeed set us free is Christlike, even when—perhaps especially when—the truth is "I am wonderful!"

It has been my experience that more people suffer from a negative perception of self than are endangered by an exaggerated positive image of themselves. Of course both are possible but it is important to note that surrendering to the truth means surrendering to the positive truth as well as a negative.

In the song "Amazing Grace," there is a phrase: "...that saved a wretch like me." I have a friend who will not sing it. She explained that after fifty years of trudging through the layers of enculturation to her target of self-awareness she has finally discovered she is not a wretch and she will not proclaim that she is. "I have been unaware many times and out of that unawareness I have harmed others and myself. I have judged people, gossiped about them, lashed out at my husband and children at times when I was frustrated with myself. I have done many things I wish I had not done. But the more aware I become, the more I understand myself and heal, the less I act in sinful ways. I do not deny that I have acted against God, myself and others and caused pain in this world. But through awareness I have learned that I am not a bad person. I am at times a wounded person and an unaware person who reacts in unkind, reactionary ways. But I have found the truth that at my very core God and I are one. The closer I grow toward my center, the closer I get to God, and the more I know that I am *not* a wretch!"

Jesus has told us that the truth will set us free. Yes, indeed it will, but only if we courageously surrender to it even if our whole congregation is singing a different tune.

A mentor of mine reminded me in a letter to always stick to my own path and my own truth rather than pure conditioning. He cautioned me to always remain "fearless and free." In fearlessness and freedom, he told me, you will find the spiritual peace that is already inside you. He was right.

I Am-ness

These insights—my friend's discovery that she was not a wretch and my mentor's understanding that freedom is always more important to spiritual maturity than conditioning—are part of the theory of "I am-ness." I began to understand this as I thought about a philosophical definition of the concept of essence. Essence is that after which nothing else could be taken away. I began to think of the ways so many of us define ourselves. I made a list:

Our jobs
Our financial status
Our relationships
Our race
Our religion
Our physical appearance
Our family names or status

The list could be endless. But what are we in our essence? What are we after everything that is nonessential is taken away? What is left? If we lose our job, do we still exist at our essential level? Yes. If we lose our money, is our essence the same? Yes. Down the list I went asking the same question, "If this somehow changed would our essence still exist?" I always came to the same conclusion. Yes. Even if our very physical life is lost, if our hearts stop beating, does our essence still exist? In faith, my answer was still yes. So I wondered who am I, what am I essentially if all the items on my list were ultimately nonessential? The answer seemed obvious. I am. That of course is the way God defined himself to Moses, "I AM WHO AM." That is what we are at our center. That is what we are at our core.

When we act contrary to this sacred reality, it is because we are unaware of the truth of our essence. One of my students wrote about the creator and creation as the big "I am" and the little "I am"s. In whatever way we choose to imagine it, the truth is there for us in awesome simplicity. We are sacred. We are created in the image and likeness of God. Though we may often mistake nonessentials for our deepest identity, we are one with God at our center, where we can rest and enjoy the peace that is beyond understanding. I am convinced that the great "I am" waits for us to surrender to the truth of our essence. Our restless hearts which, as Saint Augustine said, can only find rest in God, can take comfort in the fact that the rest we seek is available to us. God's voice is calling us home to the center of ourselves and to our I am-ness.

One of the things I most appreciate about my Catholic religious heritage is the writings of the mystics. From every era in the Church's history we have a treasure of insights from some of the world's greatest spiritual masters. What I find most appealing about mystics like Teresa of Avila, Saint John of the Cross, Meister Eckhart, Hildegard of Bingen, Thomas Merton and so many others is the consistent message that God, ourselves and others are, ultimately, one. Many find this message confusing, contradicting other religious tenets. The limits of human language and knowledge are apparent here. Many spiritual experiences are difficult to articulate. There is much that is mystery. I am often reminded of the student who asked me, "If Jesus was really God, to whom was he talking when he was praying?" When we began our discussion, we defined surrender as knowing that we are not God, but the mystics tell us we are one with God. How can we reconcile these ideas?

The concept of oneness does not claim that we as individuals are the creator of the universe and the ultimate power in creation. We are believing that we are so intimately in union with God at our core that we cannot be separated from our divine birthright.

Blinded by our illusions, we see ourselves as separate from God and others. But when the illusions fall away, we are left with the awesome truth: At our core we are the essence of "I am," and so is everyone else. It is a sacred privilege, then, for us to seek our center. In doing that we are seeking God. In seeking to understand others and see them beyond our conditioning, prejudice and judgments, we are seeking God.

The Four Basic Cultures

The four basic cultures are the key elements which make up our enculturation. When we reflect upon the ways in which we have been conditioned by our experiences, it is especially helpful to look at these cultures and analyze the impact they may have on the way we perceive ourselves and the world. Keep in mind that everyone is the product of some conditioning, and some conditioning is positive and worth keeping; other aspects of our conditioning may be better surrendered.

Remember, most people live on the "outer edges" of self-awareness. The world is filled with reactionary thinkers. Where do the automatic reactions of so many come from? Consider the four basic cultures and how your own unique versions of these have affected your life. That understanding will help you grow in self-awareness and make surrender more real for you.

Think of surrender as the bridge between the outermost layers of self-knowledge and the center of ourselves where peace and personal freedom are. Self-awareness can be seen as the material out of which the bridge of surrender is made, step by step, brick by brick. Acquiring an understanding of our four basic cultures brings us closer to a life of peace. Remember that surrender can mean the difference between suffering and misery. We know that there are no guarantees that we can avoid suffering in this life, but based on the spiritual principles of every world religion, we need not be in misery. We can, like Saint Paul, be in the midst of some of life's greatest challenges and still have a solid inner peace. He called it the peace that passes all understanding.

Surrender brings that peace. Let's look at some of those bricks that build our bridge of surrender, aid in self-awareness and lead us to peace.

Personal Enculturation. Personal enculturation has two facets: One is biological and chemical; the other is emotional and psychological. Our personal cultures have enormous influence in our lives. Personal culture is made up of all of the experiences and circumstances of our lives. It is also comprised of our own biochemistry and the ways in which that may influence us through our attitudes, behavior and moods.

Scientists and medical professionals are just beginning to realize the impact of biochemistry on moods and behavior. Many are afflicted with hormone or blood-sugar imbalances or abnormalities in brain chemistry which can cause depression, anxiety or mood swings. Take time to objectively investigate your own physical circumstances. If you do not feel that you are affected by an imbalance in biochemistry, remember two things:

1) It is possible to be affected by biological factors and not know it. As you progress in self-discovery, keep in mind the possible influence of an imbalance in biochemistry.

2) It can be tempting to judge others whose behavior clearly seems wrong to us. But, we can never be sure whether they have the ability to act differently, to understand that their behavior is harmful or to see the truth of their behavior objectively. Even if we are blessed with good mental and physical health, we must not assume that everyone else has the same advantage. We can walk a mile in someone else's shoes, but we can never understand what it is like to live inside their skin.

I am reminded of the emphasis that the Puritans put on the sin of laziness. Many historians see a direct connection with the Puritan's disdain for laziness and the "work ethic" which is such a strong part of the history and culture of the United States. The Puritans did not have the medical information we have available to us, but I have wondered how many people living in their era (or our own) were criticized for being lazy when, in fact, they may have suffered from a malfunctioning thyroid. How easy it is to judge others!

Can all this emphasis on body chemistry and psychology (rather than good old-fashioned sin) make some people excuse their bad behavior by inappropriately blaming body chemistry or past abuse? Yes, of course that can happen. I am sure it does. But the fact that some may misuse information does not mean the rest of us should not use it. Certainly there are people who could use material from this book or any other to allow themselves to hide from responsibility, but we have no control over that. I am convinced that, in the long run, it does not matter. Those who want to avoid the trip inward can find ample excuses. If you do not want to see the objective truth about yourself— you won't. If you do, you must consider all the variables. While giving workshops on surrender, I have rarely had an occasion when someone did not voice concern that these spiritual principles could be misused. One man asked why I didn't tell a schoolgirl who betrayed her friend that she had sinned and broken God's law. I responded by asking if he thought that response would have helped her to understand why she did what she did, helping her to avoid such behavior in the future. "But you are excusing her of moral responsibility," he fumed. "You let her get away with a terrible sin and gave her psycho-babble." I explained to him that I did not consider it my role to count her sins or anyone else's. I also explained that this girl was judging herself more harshly than I ever could. Surrender is a Christian principle that is not negotiable. The spiritual life of the Christian is based, both in Scripture and tradition, on authentically surrendering one's life to God. I simply did not believe that calling that girl a sinner would have done anything to help her grow toward surrender. I also pointed out that my assigning judgment to her would not be helpful in my own attempts to live a surrendered life.

I appreciated the fact that this concerned man was so interested in the topic but within the context of a workshop he and I were not able to reach any kind of harmonious thinking on this matter. Eventually I said to him with honesty and genuine respect for his concern that I thought he should just ignore me and what I was saying. What I was saying was causing him great distress and the more we talked the more distressed he became. Emotional violence of any kind done to the self or others is never appropriate. I did not have an investment in whether he agreed with me or not. I believe if one's distress over the discussion of a spiritual issue clearly causes discomfort to the point where someone is feeling a form of emotional violence it is best to drop the issue. The issue will be around if you want to come back to it at a later time. Don't force yourself to see someone's view if to do so would be emotionally violent for you. Don't try to force someone else to see your view. That is just another form of emotional violence. Force is the key in this situation.

If while discussing religious issues voices begin to rise and emotions become strained, drop the discussion. You can always come back to it later. What did it matter if at that moment this gentleman and I agreed about a spiritual teaching? If he did not like what I was saying after a reasonable period of discussion I truly believe he should just ignore me and follow his own insight. If either one of our views change, fine. If not, fine. Healthy surrender is always more important than proving a religious point. If we are serious about taking the inward journey and the point at issue is a block to the journey, it will resurface. We can deal with it later when it is less distressing.

It should be pointed out that in speaking about the effects of enculturation I am not dismissing civil responsibilities. If someone commits a violent crime the spiritual principles of self-awareness would not interfere in a society's obligation to protect itself and imprison the criminal. Civil issues are not the focus of this book. Noting that a malfunctioning thyroid could cause someone to appear lazy is not the same as absolving criminals from their crimes. It should not be thought of as a step leading to reduced prison sentences or a new rash of nonguilty verdicts because the defendant lacked self-awareness. I have rarely given a workshop when someone did not express alarm that the concepts of sin or civil responsibility were being eroded. In some groups I have been stunned by the persistence of people who try to connect these ancient spiritual principles with their fear of social violence or the loss of cultural concepts with which they are comfortable.

In our investigation into the concept of surrender, the focus is on spiritual maturity. Regardless of whether someone else misuses the principles we should simply ask ourselves if we see a value in following them. Remember Jesus telling people to take the plank out of their own eye before worrying about the splinter in someone else's eye? Many of my workshop participants readily agree with these principles until the topic of crime is raised. There is a tendency to resist to applying these principles to those who have committed acts which we all agree are objectively wrong. My response is always the same: Yes, civic and social institutions need to make decisions about crime and criminals. Yes, there are some people who, due to their violence (or extreme acting out from their own emotional damage), should not roam freely about the population. But we must remember that those who commit crimes also have an essence, modes of thought, cultural conditioning and a target of self-awareness. Though it may be difficult to accept, criminals who are not seriously mentally ill (violently psychotic or sociopathic) have just as much potential to realize self-awareness as any of us. For most of us, though, the rehabilitation of criminals is not one of our primary concerns. The teaching of Jesus is clear enough. Most of us have planks in our eyes and one of our primary spiritual tasks is to remove those planks. We learn to do that by understanding the psychological and emotional impact of personal enculturation.

Personal culture is like a fingerprint. No one in the world ever has had or ever will have your exact personal culture. Even if you have a twin and you have been very close and notice remarkable similarities in personal habits as well as physical features, you do not share the same personal culture.

Were you an only child? One child out of ten? Was your family warm and loving or did your parents struggle with emotional damage from their lives and bring the result of the damage into your home? What about the other children at your school? Did you feel accepted? Did you struggle academically? Were your teachers influential in positive or negative ways? Were you physically healthy? Perhaps you experienced a hospitalization as a young child. How might that have affected you and your perceptions?

Write an autobiography, see a counselor, draw a personal culture tree with the major experiences of your life, influential people or important conversations as branches. You may be amazed by what you find yourself focusing on. It may not be what you expect. Ask for input from others who may have a different memory of the same event. But, before you begin, make a promise that you will not judge yourself. Venting emotional violence on ourselves only delays the surrender process. We are not looking for right or wrong here—only awareness. If you are especially upset by memories of some events, that may be your clue that you need to walk this path with someone else—talk through it with a friend or counselor.

Look at yourself as someone new you have just met. You want to understand all you can about this new person in your life. You just want to understand, not judge or categorize. The influence of your family, friends, neighborhood, financial status, the death of someone close, your health or that of someone you loved—anything and everything you can remember are clues to your thoughts and behavior today. Perhaps you are the product of your conditioning or, perhaps, you have considered these things before and have made a conscious decision to *not* simply be the product of conditioning. But there is always more God may want to show you about yourself or others—reflect again.

I had a wonderful teacher who said that, in order to see the difference between our conditioning and our choices, we should think of our life as a car trip. We may think that we make the decisions about whether to go fast or slow, turn right or left. But most of our "cars" are so full of the voices of our parents, teachers, peer groups and experiences that we are not making many free choices at all. My teacher suggested that we should stop our cars, get out and yell, "OK everybody out," then hop back in, roll up the windows and lock the doors. Then we can decide which events and people (in terms of their influence over us) we will let back in. I wrote down the following examples in my note pad:

"OK, Grandma, remember when you told me that it was good to trust people, but that blind faith was not using the gift of intelligence God gave me? I see the truth of that now. Thank you, Granny. I appreciate your wisdom. You can get back in."

"OK, fourth-grade teacher, remember when you told me that I was lazy and that my printing was not fit for an infant? You were wrong to say that. I disagree and I do not want you in my car or on my trip. You are out for good. Take a taxi."

I once had a student come to my office insisting that I change his grade from a B to an A. He paced around my office, near hysteria. He told me that he had to have an A because he had to get into medical school and he could not compete without straight A's. Then he said something common sense should have told him not to say: In anger and frustration he admitted he did not earn an A and said, "Oh, come on, give me a break. It is only theology." (Perhaps not the best argument to make to a theology teacher.) I tried to calm him down and asked him what it was about medicine that made him so anxious to study it and spend his life building a career in it. He replied that he just *had* to be a doctor! His father was a doctor! His brothers were doctors! He absolutely *had* to get into medical school and become a doctor.

I felt very bad for him, and have remembered him over the years. I remember thinking, "Whose life are you living? Have you ever made any free choices about your life?" I wonder about him sometimes. I suspect that somewhere he is now a doctor practicing medicine. I also wonder if he—the *essential* he—has any interest whatsoever in medicine. Self-awareness could have kept this young man from following a road map designed for someone else. He may have needed a lot of courage to follow his own path and his own truth but that is precisely the point—it would have been his. (By the way, the grade he earned was a *B*, and he received a *B*.)

Long before I studied theology I was a third-grade teacher. One day on the playground I found a war of sorts among the seventh-grade girls. The night before, one of the girls in their clique, Linda, had asked her friend Alice if she would keep a secret. Alice promised she would. Linda unburdened herself, telling Alice that she had been experiencing serious abuse within her family. The two girls cried and hugged each other and promised to be friends forever. But the next day before noon, Alice had told the secret to the entire seventh grade. Emotions ran high. Shouting and crying followed and girls began to choose sides.

After quieting them down I asked Alice to come and talk with me. I asked her why she had betrayed her friend when she had promised she wouldn't. She broke into heaving sobs and exclaimed, "I don't know why I did it. I really don't." And she did not know. She had no idea. Even without knowing her, you might be able to guess what was behind this terrible behavior. As we talked, Alice told me that she had never really felt important in her group of friends. She was in constant fear that they would reject her. I pointed out to her that out of all the girls in the group her friend Linda had chosen her to share such an important and serious secret. I told her that certainly gave me the impression that Linda considered her very special. She was astonished. "Yes, I guess so," was her response.

Later, she concluded that, before she realized what she was doing, she found herself savoring the opportunity to be the most important person in the group because she knew a secret. And for the minute it took to tell the secret, she felt special and important. Everyone's attention was on her. Of course, after she realized what she had done and saw the look of horror on Linda's face, she felt worse than ever about herself and actually created what she feared most—she was being rejected by a number of the girls.

It is frightening to realize the amount of pain a lack of self-knowledge can cause, even for seventh-graders. Alice had in fact been considered an important member of her social group. Her fears that she would be rejected by the others came from some other experience and she unconsciously projected that onto her peer group. She learned something very important from the whole episode, but not until she had deeply hurt her friend. Although she had done a horrible thing, Alice was not a bad or hateful girl. She was overwhelmed by her conditioning, unaware of why she acted the way she did. Perhaps her dramatic glimpse into herself so early helped her avoid falling into such behavior again.

The impact of the different areas of our personal enculturation is impossible to calculate. One day, I made up a story in my college classroom designed to show how our reactions might be based upon what is already in us, not on present circumstances. I asked the students to suppose they were all aspiring writers and I was the writing teacher. What if I returned graded papers to the students and said to some, "You will never be a writer. You should change your major. You just do not have what it takes"? I could almost assure the class that different students would react differently based more on their personal enculturation and conditioning than on what I—the supposed expert—said on that particular day. One student would consider what I said and then bring her paper to several other people, seeking other opinions. Perhaps she would write other papers and seek input from many people, trying to come to her own conclusion. Another student may feel driven to succeed by what I said. (I call this sort the "you just watch me" kind of people.) He may drive himself to writing success just to prove that I was wrong. Our society would generally applaud him, but we should ask if he spent a lifetime writing out of bondage to the inconsiderate remark of one teacher or out of his own free choice. It seems to me there are a lot of people that society may consider successful who live very far from personal freedom and do not enjoy the peace it offers.

The final example I gave was about a student who would crumble in defeat after such a response. She might never allow anyone to see a story she had written again. She would be so devastated by the harshness and negativity of that one response that she would hand her dreams over to her critical teacher and let go of them in an unhealthy form of surrender. That type of surrender would come from woundedness and illusion, not truth and strength.

After I finished my made-up examples I talked to the students about what they thought had more influence over my imaginary students—the teacher's opinion or their own enculturation. As I finished I mentioned my hope that a real teacher would not behave in such a way. As soon as I said that, one of my students, a thirty-five-year-old freshman, told me that a real teacher most certainly would do something like that. She had almost the exact experience of the harsh teacher's comments when she was a senior in high school. "I was like the last example you gave," she told us. "I just crumbled. I wanted to go to college, but I was devastated after a teacher told me I was not a very creative person—she questioned whether I was 'college material'." She added that she knew the teacher's comments did not make sense because she made very good grades in high school, but she was paralyzed with fear. Finally she said, "I am a freshman at this age for only one reason: that teacher, or rather the power I gave to that teacher and her opinions. My parents wanted me to go to college and would have paid for it. Later, my husband would have supported my decision to go to school. I just could not bring myself until now to face the possibility that that teacher was wrong."

I was stunned, not only because the student's story so closely resembled my made-up example, but also by how frequently and consistently I see people living their lives out of an illusion planted by someone else. At the end of that semester I noted that the student who had so bravely returned to school despite her fears was, in fact, an excellent student. She was intelligent and creative, and she turned in a final term paper far superior to most in the class. I was relieved to know that even though it took her a number of years she had finally told her high school teacher to take her inappropriate opinions and get out of her car!

Religious Enculturation. Religious enculturation refers to the way our religious background has affected our thoughts and perspectives. It is most obvious in the religious tradition we grew up in. Clearly, those who attended church, religious instruction, Bible camps or church school, have been influenced by the messages we received in our religious training.

What we have discovered though is that, for most of us, the strongest impact of religious conditioning comes from the very earliest messages we received regarding God, our relationship to God and religious concepts such as sin, heaven, hell and being "saved."

It may be difficult for you to remember back to those earliest messages but, if possible, try to get in touch with the memory of the first time God was explained to you.

Were you warned in a threatening voice that even if your parents could not watch you every minute God would see you (so you would not think you were going to get away with anything)? Was your first view of God that of a policeman in the sky? Or, were you told that you were God's greatest creation? One parishioner said her grandmother told her that God did his very finest work when he created her granddaughter. "I know that is a very grandmotherly thing to say," she allowed. "But from that day when I was four or five until this one I have always felt on some very deep level that God was proud of me. After all, I was his greatest work!"

One day, my four-year-old nephew was sitting very still, not moving his head or face. Yet he kept darting his eyes quickly upward and then down again. Up and then down again.

"What are you doing?" I finally asked him.

"I am trying to catch God," he said.

He went on to explain that his mother had told him that

God lives in heaven beyond the clouds. So he began "looking" for God by watching the sky. He thought perhaps he would see God, "coming home or something." When that method didn't work, he decided that God must not want to be seen. When I saw him darting his eyes around, it was because he was trying to catch God off-guard. He was determined to get just a quick glimpse of God even if the object of his search was a bit hard to track down.

Family members got a kick out of the story. It was only years later that I realized how the story of my nephew's search for God can give us insights into the ways young children hear religious comments given to them. Early messages about religion and the spiritual life are a very significant part of our enculturation. Can you remember early comments or attitudes that were passed along to you regarding God and other religious topics? What happened to those earliest concepts?

One woman told me that she had been very ill as a young child. She was hospitalized and frightened about being away from her parents overnight. The sights and sounds of the hospital were equally frightening. Her mother told her that God would be there to watch over her when her parents could not. So, her first image of God was that of an invisible parent who would protect her. Later in her hospital stay, her aunt came to visit. In her attempt to be comforting she said, "I know it is difficult, dear, but we must believe that God has his reasons for allowing this to happen."

"Suddenly I was filled with anger," she said. "I was comfortable with the notion that God was a kind of invisible babysitter. But my aunt's comments that God had his reasons suddenly struck a chord: God was responsible for my illness, the hospitalization, for everything bad! I didn't say anything to anyone, but I decided that I didn't like God anymore. If he had his reasons for hurting children and making their parents cry, that meant he did it. He caused all of our pain. God was not to be trusted. I have reflected upon that event so many years ago and have had many new images of God since, but I must admit that I still struggle with the notion of God causing all the pain in my life. It's like the concept has been hard-wired into my brain."

Have you ever wondered how a number of people can hear a particular sermon and yet they all hear different things? Remember, all areas of our enculturation overlap and affect each other. You may have a former classmate from a Catholic grade school. Even though you both attended the same parish, you do not have exactly the same religious enculturation. You both were given different messages by your parents and your lives have not been identical.

Take time to consider the different areas of your religious enculturation. Consider the ways in which your personal enculturation may have influenced your religious enculturation, and vice versa. How have your earliest religious experiences colored the way you look at life today? Do you still feel that your early concepts of God are valid? If not, how can you understand God differently?

Ethnic and National Enculturation. Each of us belongs to an ethnic and national group, and this, too, influences our experience of the world. If you are from the United States, for example, you probably feel that a majority opinion on an issue should prevail in both government and religious issues. Of course, there is a diversity of opinion in every nation, but it is surprising how strong our national conditioning can be.

As an example, in the United States it is easy to find studies determining the breakdown of Catholics' opinions on any given Church issue. We know the Catholic Church is not set up as a democratic system. There are Catholics all over the world, many from cultures very different from ours, most of whom have no interest in calculating the latest percentages of Catholics for or against an issue. On several occasions, I have heard Catholics from France or Bolivia or South Africa make good-natured jibes about how Catholics in the United States are "obsessed" with poll-taking. It is much easier to notice the national conditioning of other people than to be aware of our own. Still, with some reflection, some of the more obvious elements of your national conditioning will become apparent.

When I lived in Peru for a time I became especially aware of the many ways that I have been conditioned by growing up in the United States. Until I began to travel and actually spend some time living in other countries, I never realized how attached I was to the way of life in the United States. One day I went to the post office in Lima. It was very crowded and I was shocked to find people pushing and elbowing their way to the front window. There were no neat lines where people held little white pieces of paper with numbers on them. There was no concept of first come, first served—like we did it in the Midwest. And the only people besides me who seemed to be disconcerted by the relative disorder were other people from the United States! After a while, we learned to laugh at ourselves and our expectations and push our way to the front like everyone else.

Again, when I went to a movie theater in Lima, I saw signs prohibiting smoking. Anyone who smoked would be asked to leave the theater, they said. But all over the theater people were smoking and no one seemed to mind—except people from the United States. Most of us were annoyed and shocked. When I pointed this situation out to a native friend, she laughed, "Oh, you Gringos!" she teased, "You are all alike. Don't be so nervous about some silly sign. Just live your life."

So in just the first few days of experiencing another culture it becomes clear just how much a product of conditioning we can be—even those of us who try to be reflective.

When some of my Peruvian friends returned from a visit to the United States, they gave me some of their impressions. I was astounded when one of them said they never expected the United States to be so rigid and legalistic, especially given its reputation as a free society. Confused, I had to ask what they had found so legalistic and rigid. They recited a list: "Don't bring that dog in here. It's the law! Wear a helmet. It's the law! Don't smoke here. It's the law. Don't throw paper on the street. It's the law." The list went on and on. They were amazed, not only at all the unnecessarily strict rules, but also that so many people followed them. They told me of an experience they had at the theater. Two people in the group didn't like the show, so they went out to the lobby, sat on a step and began to talk very quietly. Shortly after, a guard politely told them they were not allowed to sit there—it was against the fire code. One of them asked, "Do you really think that if there is a fire we are going to continue to sit on this step?" The guard told them that he was sorry but they would have to move. It was the law!

I would never have considered any of those laws rigid. In fact, I was not really even conscious of those laws. I followed them and basically agreed with them. I was unaware of how much I took those cultural attitudes for granted. Without the experience of friends from a different culture I would still be totally unaware of these aspects of my national enculturation. Once I returned home I was conscious of "It's the law" being everywhere. I still feel that most of these laws are good for us, so I have no problem just incorporating them into my life. But I can now understand how people from other cultures might find them excessive and annoying.

Our national and ethnic cultures can condition our attitudes toward rules and regulations as well as our understanding of how to behave politely, how to express love—even an understanding of what love is. Appropriate dress, body language, eye contact, even appropriate behavior while shopping and eating in restaurants are all determined by our culture. Ultimately, for our purposes, we want to become aware of the ways in which our national and ethnic conditioning may have influenced our understanding of God.

It may seem that there is little connection between another country's way of running a post office and our religious ideas, but looked at in the broad sense of the formation of attitudes and expectations it is possible that any of our conditioning may find its way into our interpretations. For some of us, ethnic enculturation may have a bigger influence than for others. Some people easily identify with a minority ethnic group because circumstances have forced them to be aware of their minority status; others do so because of a strong family identity with their ethnicity. However, recognizing your ethnic background is not the same as being truly conscious of the ways in which that ethnicity has influenced your general attitudes and expectations. Since each ethnic group has its own unique history and culture, sometimes even including smaller groups, becoming aware of our ethnic influences may be a long process.

I was in graduate school before I understood how much I had been influenced by the fact that I came from many generations of IrishCatholicDemocrats. No hyphens here— I grew up seeing this as one big group. Later, I studied the Irish-American immigrants who came to St. Louis, Missouri (my hometown), and found that many of them immigrated because they were uneducated and sought jobs in the many sweat shops here. Because the city was built on the Mississippi River, and products were shipped up and down the river, St. Louis became a popular place for new immigrants looking for work. I was fascinated to find out that in the Irish neighborhood known as Kerry Patch in turn-of-the-century St. Louis there were specific religious groups among the Catholics. One group tended to be very pious, somewhat superstitious and very strict in their regular practice of the faith. Another group within the same Irish Catholic neighborhood also considered themselves good strong Catholics but tended to be much more independent in their religious views. This second group also tended to be much more open with their criticism of Church authority. It would not have been uncommon for members of this second group to say publicly that they disagreed with the parish priest on some issue and that they were confident in their own view, which scandalized the first, more pious, group. Yet both groups considered themselves good Catholics.

I am descended from the second, more opinionated group. As I studied about the lives and attitudes of my ethnic group, I realized how much of their characteristics were present in my mother. For example, one Friday evening before the Second Vatican Council revoked the ban on meat on Friday, my sister and I came home to find my mother making hot dogs for dinner. As good Catholic schoolchildren, we quickly reminded our mother that it was Friday and we could not eat meat.

"Oh my gosh! I completely forgot it was Friday!" my mother said. "Oh well, the food is cooked. Go ahead and eat what I've fixed."

Upset, my sister and I insisted we could not possibly eat those hot dogs. Our teachers had told us that eating meat on Friday was a sin. We could not eat that meat! After a few minutes of our protests my mother slapped her hand down on the kitchen table with a loud *whop*. Looking us straight in the eyes she said, "Listen! When you get to heaven, if God says anything about these hot dogs, *you tell him to talk to me!*"

My sister and I learned a few lessons that evening (and on other similar occasions) that I can see threaded throughout my theological responses to my studies and Church involvement. In the language of the time of the Hot Dog Incident I learned (was conditioned to believe) that the Church's laws could be overturned by my mother and that it was a good idea to consider all further religious teaching carefully before I claimed it as my own. My grandmother once told me that it was a sin not to use the brain God gave you to make up your own mind regarding a topic as important as religion. Both my mother and grandmother would have been offended had anyone suggested that they were not good Catholics. In their minds, though, being a good Catholic sometimes included disagreeing with the institutional Church.

Since then, I have tried to step back from my conditioning and see things from other sides. I have even completed the assignment I give my students, asking them to argue for a position opposite to their own. Over the years I have found I disagree with many of the viewpoints my family members held. I made a decision to leave many of those attitudes outside my "car" as I drove away. Yet, there are other family views—especially religious and political— that I found I kept returning to and agreeing with. I invited those ideas into my car and have traveled many miles with them, always trying to be open to views that may change my perspective. It is truly amazing how much we can be connected to the lives and attitudes of people that we did not even know. Sometimes I wonder about all those residents of "Kerry Patch"—I think how many of them have influenced me and I don't even know their names. When thinking about the past, it is most important to know how it influences your present and to decide if you choose to keep the influence in your life.

Present Enculturation. Present enculturation is just what it sounds like. You are part of the culture of the present moment. Political events, cultural ideas, songs, movies and books all have some influence over the culture they are a part of. It is important for all of us to consider the ways in which our present culture affects us.

I recently heard a group of fourth-graders discussing AIDS, including a rather clinical discussion of safe-sex practices. I was astonished. I could hardly believe that a group of children so young would be having such a frank, even clinical discussion and there was no giggling or childish behavior in response to the topic. One of the girls in the group had an uncle who was dying from advanced AIDS. Such discussions were common in her home and she shared her family discussions. It seemed these children had lost some of their innocence, but I realized that AIDS was part of their present culture. Aside from the information that one classmate related to them, they lived in a world where safe-sex commercials were on TV. Movies about AIDS were in theaters and on TV as well. Many schools have initiated frank discussions about the disease. When I was in fourth grade what we knew about sex was limited and met with giggles, snickers and some discomfort. As I stood listening to this group seriously discussing the possible relationship between sex and death, I could only wonder about the influence of their present culture on their adult life. Of course AIDS is in my present culture as well, but it became an issue in the culture after I was adult. Present culture influences need to be considered in any assessment of enculturation. What was the culture like when you were a child? a teenager? a young adult? How has the particular time in which you have lived affected your interpretations and attitudes?

CHAPTER SIX

❀

The Cycle of Interpretation

The cycle of interpretation is another helpful aid in learning about ourselves, making it easier to live lives of surrender. There are three basic stages to the cycle of interpretation:

Diagram of the three stages

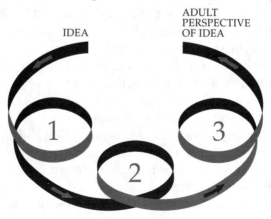

IDEA

ADULT
PERSPECTIVE
OF IDEA

1

2

3

Stage One: Childhood

Stage one is called childhood. These stages are not necessarily related to chronological age. They are correlated to our ability to interpret things open-mindedly and, when necessary, with an attitude of surrender. Therefore, the first stage has less to do with your age than with your level of self-awareness and ability to think critically. Like children, the one who acts from this stage does so without critical analysis or serious reflection. Such people tend to just accept what they are told, without question. Like the interpretive habits of very young children, this stage can be dangerous.

If someone tells a child repeatedly he is stupid or unwanted, the child will most likely believe it, regardless of the objective truth. This first-stage information, whether true or not, can become the truth in the mind of a child or anyone who tends to interpret things from the first stage.

Stage Two: Adolescence

The second stage is called adolescence. As in chronological adolescence people who interpret from this stage are caught between two other stages. Adolescents are not children, yet they are not adults. Those who are in stage two of the cycle of interpretation are not in the non-reflective stage one, but they are not in the surrendered, adult interpretation state of stage three. This can make stage two a very confusing, even painful, place to be.

Let's walk through an example of someone's cycles of interpretation. Although these stages are not necessarily related to chronological age, our example coincidentally overlaps the literal ages for childhood and adolescence. Suppose a mother tells her small child, "God will always be there for you." I am purposely using a rather obscure phrase because it is open to so many interpretations. When the child hears that God will always be there for him, he interprets that message in his six-year-old mind. "Great," he thinks, "God will always be here for me. That means I will get whatever I want for Christmas, no mean kids will pick on me and everything will be wonderful." Because a six-year-old does not reflect upon the meaning of his mother's message, he will simply store it and label it "the truth." That is, until something comes along to challenge "the truth."

Now our example child is fourteen. His mother is in the hospital and she is very sick. The young man hears people whisper that his mother may die. Reaching back to what he has lodged in his brain's filing system under the heading "God" is his belief that God will always be there for him. "Alright, God," he thinks, "Now is the time for you to really be here for me and for my Mom. Don't let her die. I am counting on you God. I know you will be here now that I need you. Don't let my Mom die." The young man prays based on his understanding of God from his first stage. But what happens when his mother does indeed die? Naturally, the young man is heartbroken and it is likely he is also angry at God. He had an interpretation of God given to him by his mother herself. God failed him. God failed his mother. God was certainly not "there" for him when he needed it most.

Now our young interpreter is hurled into the midst of stage two. He may feel lost. He no longer knows what or if to believe. He is angry and confused. What had been an innocent and naive first-stage interpretation has turned into confusion, perhaps even depression. First he experienced the loss of his mother, and now he has lost his concept of God as well.

When you hit the second stage, maybe because of a conversation, reflective thoughts, or an event such as the mother's death in our example, your original first-stage interpretations are challenged. When you leave the first stage, especially if your interpretations are harshly challenged, the second stage can be, at first, a place of anger and confusion. You are no longer in the apparent safety and security of stage one, yet you have not arrived at the new, adult interpretation of stage three.

When your first-stage concepts are exposed to doubt, there are three ways to interpret those thoughts or events that challenge your earliest notions:

1) Denial. If the new information is too painful or uncomfortable to look at, some people will choose to stay in stage one, refusing to acknowledge the new information which could create new interpretations. If, for example, a woman believed she was in love (from a conditioned, first-stage perspective), she may be hesitant to think critically about what she begins to recognize as emotional cruelty on the part of her beloved. She may, after being exposed to the second stage of interpretation, just turn around and go back to the first stage, insisting to herself and others that her love is wonderful and there are no problems. In the case of the young man who lost his mother, he may feel the need to hold on to his first-stage understanding of God, even though he senses that this interpretation no longer fits his experience.

2) Anger. The second option is to build a brick house of anger and move in. Anger and, often, confusion come with the second stage of adolescence, causing us to refuse to move beyond it.

I witnessed the rage of a talk-show host complaining about his lost respect for the Roman Catholic Church—he had held on to his anger for almost thirty years! He had apparently had a strong, but naive, first-stage interpretation of the Church. His interpretation was seriously challenged when he realized the faults and failings of the human community of the Church and he was unable to let go of his shock and anger. He was severely disappointed because he had been led to believe there should not have been so much sin in the Church!

Everyone is vulnerable to the brokenness that results in sin. Our talk-show host vented his disappointment with the Church on numerous occasions during the run of his popular TV show. By the last ten years of his show, I hardly recognized the mostly pre-Vatican II Church to which he referred. He was frustrated and disgusted with the reality of the Church, rather than realizing the inadequacies of his first-stage interpretation. I must admit that during the first few years of his tirade against the sins of the Church I was comfortable with his emotional comments. I thought it was probably healthy for him to speak openly about the Church and its problems. But when those first several years turned into five years, then ten, twenty and finally nearly thirty, it struck me that this man's anger was more hurtful than helpful for both him and the Church at large. In order to surrender in a situation like this, he would have to let go of his anger and disappointment. Whether he eventually chose to remain a member of the Church or not, a reassessment of his original vision of the Church, a surrender to the reality of human communities and an eventual reinterpretation of his stage-one views would have, most likely, allowed him to spend fewer years in anger and more years in peaceful acceptance—not of what is unacceptable in terms of failures in integrity if he could not have somehow been part of changing those faults—but of what had already happened and could not be changed. Perhaps he could have even seen through his anger at some point and seen the positive aspects of the Church. For that to happen, however, he would have had to accept what he could not change about the one billion members of the Roman Catholic Church.

3) Surrender and Reinterpretation. The third option you have after finding yourself in the second stage of the cycles of interpretation is to analyze what you have experienced so far and be willing to surrender previous interpretations and move on to a new, less naive, more adult interpretation.

Stage Three: Surrender

The third stage of the cycle is possible to experience only after you have surrendered any clutching and clinging that may have been a part of our first or second stages. Let go—and remain open to new information. Reaching the third stage comes without any expectations. If you believed you had a trusted and honorable friend and circumstances proved otherwise, decisions regarding what to do with the friendship (Do I remain in contact with this person? Do I stop the relationship?) are less important than the interpretive cycle and level of awareness from which we make the decision. Third-stage interpretations are based on awareness, surrendering past interpretations and being willing to deal with reality.

To go back to our example, the young man who found himself in the second stage after the death of his mother could experience the peace of the third stage in several ways. They all included passing through surrender. Once having expressed his anger at God, and/or his mother for "misleading" him in his original concept of God, the young man could reinterpret the possible meanings of the phrase "be there for you." He could seek guidance about his understanding of God as well as his anger and loss. When he is able to let go of what he cannot change, he will be free to move on to another, more adult, stage of interpretation. The third-stage interpretation is based on what one can know about the objective truth, a letting go of expectations and a willingness to be open to new and different ideas. Our young believer just may find a much deeper and more comforting concept of God from the third stage.

The second stage is not always fraught with hardship—it may involve nothing more than a conversation or thought. Our reaction to it depends upon the issue at hand and how desperately we cling to our first-stage notions about that issue. Ultimately, moving to the third stage depends upon our willingness and ability to surrender.

We must interpret everything that happens to us

through these stages, but often we do so without really being aware of it. One of the most common ways we find ourselves experiencing the cycle of interpretation is in our cultural understanding of love. We base major, life-changing decisions on our interpretation of the complex issue of romance. Those who claim to be in love, but are working from a first-stage interpretation, are more likely to be overwhelmed by attraction, infatuation or romantic feelings. Many times during my years of college-level teaching, I heard young students proclaim they were in love, "with the perfect person" only to say shortly after that they would "never forgive" the subject of their "love" for failing them. Some simply recognized what they thought was "love" was, in fact, only attraction.

From a first-stage perspective, it is possible to mistake attraction for love, because the outlook is noncritical. From a second-stage perspective, you may see the subject of your "love" more realistically, causing you to "fall out of" love, or recognize that you had never been in love at all. Love is not, as commonly stated, "blind." There is nothing as clearsighted as true love. True love is not based upon illusion. Spiritually speaking, it would be inappropriate to use the word "love" at all until a third stage of interpretation had been reached. Love sees the faults and failings of another and loves anyway. It is important to note that this third-stage love may even cause an individual to avoid contact with the beloved if abuse or some other unhealthy element is present. Authentic love, like authentic surrender, is always based on the truth, reality and health.

A woman once told me the following story, which illustrates how vulnerable we can be to first-stage concepts of love:

> I recall a time when I felt I was in love. When some of my friends made comments like, "He seems a little immature to me," or "Can't you see how self-obsessed this guy is," I reacted with anger. How could they fail to see how perfect John was? Why would they want to destroy my dream of a wonderful life with him?

After a while, John broke off the relationship. I was hurt. For almost two years I thought of him, off and on, and each time I remembered him he became more "perfect" to me. We had had one conversation in particular that I could not forget. I replayed it in my mind (and sometimes in talking with my friends) over and over.

One of my good friends had finally had enough. She came right out and said that she could not believe that I still held this man in such high regard. She thought he was a jerk. She suggested I needed to "bust the ghost" of my memories, especially the one I played over and over. She insisted we drive to where our "perfect conversation" had taken place—she wanted to re-enact the scene. I went along with her plan, because I, too, wanted to rid myself of the nagging memories. "Is this where he sat?" my friend asked. "Yes," I responded with tears forming in my eyes. To my astonishment she began to act like a monkey! A monkey! She made faces and noises and stepped around like a silly circus monkey. I burst into laughter. I could hardly believe what she was doing. It was so unexpected and crazy. I laughed and laughed. "The ghost of this monkey is busted forever," she proclaimed. And it was. I could never sulk in that memory again, even if I had wanted to. Whenever I tried, I could only see my sophisticated, educated friend acting like a monkey.

But then, after almost two years, John called and asked me out to dinner. My friends were disgusted, but I was elated and happily accepted. Again, the most unexpected thing happened. I kept thinking, "Hmmm, didn't he use to be taller?" I sat across the table from this man of my dreams, and as he spoke I thought, "I can't believe I never realized how self-obsessed this guy is." I made a mental note not to let my friend's comments control my perspective. As I listened to him talk, I found myself wondering, "When did he become so immature?" As the dinner continued, I was in for another shock—he turned out to be a staunch conservative Republican (I am a very liberal Democrat). Yikes! I just could not believe I spent so much time "in love" with a man I knew so little about. I couldn't believe I was having dinner with a stranger, a man that I had not really known at all. Losing illusions and growing in awareness can hurt. It can also be embarrassing when the light of reality breaks through, and we realize how far from awareness we have been living. Who was the man I was so in love with? He really was perfect. And he should have been. I created him myself, in my own mind. I just borrowed someone's face and name and added the rest myself. In fact, the two men, the one in my mind and the one who legally owned the name I borrowed, were so different from each other, I still am not completely sure how I managed to be quite so creative. Had I been interpreting this man from a more mature, third-stage level of interpretation, I would have realized I did not love him. As it turned out, I didn't even really *like* him. Not only did I have to admit to my friends that I had caused my years of misery because I would not let go of my fantasy, I also realized I needed to understand enough about myself to see how I wound up in such a deep illusion. It was a difficult and painful time, but I am happy to report that I have not fallen in love with any monkeys lately!

I laughed as I appreciated the humor in her story and sighed as I caught visions of myself and my own illusions. How wonderful if we could all learn to free ourselves from the illusions that cause us so much unhappiness!

CHAPTER SEVEN

❀

Surrender and Forgiveness

One of the true joys of learning to surrender is that it becomes much easier for us to forgive others. Growing in awareness helps us to see the parts we often play in our own misery.

At times, of course, others harm us and it is not the result of our own illusions. Still, being aware that surrender can mean the difference between temporary suffering and permanent, self-inflicted misery can help us to heal even that suffering that others have caused. Realizing that the kingdom of God is within us (Luke 17), we have an inner strength we can depend upon. We cannot control what others do to us. But we do have the power to forgive them and that can free us from a lifetime of misery.

Forgiveness, like surrender, has sometimes been wrongly interpreted. Forgiving someone for the wrongs they have done to us does not mean that we lose our interest in justice. But we must trust that, when crimes have been committed against us, God is the only one who can rightfully bring a just resolution. It does us no good to nurture our anger or plan ways to strike back.

One of my favorite Gospel scenes is Jesus praying from the cross, "Father, forgive them, for they do not know what they are doing" (Luke 23:34). What a powerful lesson about surrender and forgiveness! I have always been struck by the lack of self-righteousness in this comment of Jesus. Who would have a better right to be bitter? To be accused of crimes and to be tortured would certainly constitute what most of us consider a "right" not to forgive. Yet, Jesus was not groveling in a religious way, nor did he seem to be speaking out of theological rigidity. From I am-ness, he spoke the truth he was so aware of: Those who hurt him had no idea what they were doing. That fact, of course, did not lessen the physical consequences for Jesus. It did, however, have an effect on his spiritual life and the spiritual lives of billions of other people who have been so deeply influenced by his example.

For a while, it was popular in the Church to use the phrase "Easter people." I like that idea, because it conveyed the importance of our belief in the Resurrection. Through surrender, we come to know the reality of many different kinds of resurrections in our lives and in the lives of others. People of the Resurrection know that after crucifixions of all kinds, through surrender, a resurrection follows. They know there is nothing that can control us if we are personally free and prepared, through surrender, to accept reality.

When Jesus stood before Pilate and said, "You have no power over me unless it has been given to you by the Father," he gave us another powerful lesson about the surrendered life. The power to hurt our feelings, to destroy our reputation or to do physical harm is not the ultimate power in the universe. In the life of Jesus, people like Pilate may have lived with the illusion they possessed an ultimate kind of power. Jesus saw power in this world from quite a different perspective. Even when he was sentenced to death, Jesus knew that Pilate had no real power over him.

What an awesome story of personal freedom. We may think others have power over us. We may even give them that power by imagining ourselves to be controlled by others. But Jesus taught us that only God has ultimate power. As the Psalms say, why should we fear? If God is with us, who can be against us? When we are personally free, we live in I am-ness, so intimately connected to God that we cannot be separated.

After Jesus asked the Father to forgive those who had hurt him, he said, "It is finished." In that ultimate act of letting go, he surrendered his physical life. But that death is not the purpose of his surrender; we must look beyond death, beyond our shattered illusions, to the resurrection. Lives that are broken can be repaired. Hearts that are wounded can heal. The greatest of hurts can be forgiven. For the Christian believer even the loss of physical life, another surrender, can be the beginning of a new life.

CHAPTER EIGHT

---❀---

Learning to Love the Gray

One of the most difficult items to surrender for many of us is the question "why?" We wonder why bad things happen to us. We wonder how God can allow evil things in this world. We wonder how people can be so cruel to one another. Sometimes we are able to see goodness come out of pain, but other times we see only the pain. And we want to know why. Part of surrender is realizing and accepting that, in some things, we will never have the comfort of understanding the *why* of our suffering.

There are many gray areas in human life. It is difficult to understand the behavior of others and it is impossible to completely understand God. Yet the pain of some of life's events can cause even the most self-aware people to withdraw, retreating into their anger and frustration. Often, in the midst of suffering we hear people say, "If only I could understand why!"

After we have surrendered our attempts to control

things that have hurt us, we are called to let go of the need to know the why. Think of Job: Only after he was able to surrender all of his losses—including the desire to know the whys of his suffering—was he able to experience his own resurrection and enjoy a new life.

Learning to love the gray is difficult. Like all other aspects of surrender it means we must accept what we cannot change. But we need not be afraid of the gray areas of our lives. We must keep our attention on the promise of resurrection and learn to accept that mysteries are part of every human life. Then it is possible to learn to love the gray areas in our lives as reminders that we are not God: We do not even understand the complexity of life, how much less should we expect to control it! Learning that we are part of something much bigger than ourselves can bring us relief, letting us unshoulder some of the burden we have given ourselves.

A workshop participant once gave me a little bracelet she braided out of gray ribbon. When I wear that bracelet I am reminded of how many times during the day I find myself walking in the opposite direction of surrender. I am not always instantly at peace when grappling with a new issue of "why" that has entered my life, but I have learned to love the color gray. Rather than seeing the apparent senselessness of some of our sufferings as "the salt in a wound"(as one person described it to me), I have begun to look at it as a gift. The mysterious gift of gray in my life allows me to remember I am not in my difficulties by myself and that solving all of the pain in my life and that of others is not completely up to me. What a relief!

CHAPTER NINE

———— ❀ ————

Messages and Messengers

At times, perhaps unconsciously, we may use messengers as an excuse for not going through layers of our targets of awareness and learning to acknowledge the objective truth of given situations. There are a number of ways that messengers can become stumbling blocks for us.

For some of us a pastor, spiritual director, religion teacher or author may be given far too much power by us as individuals or by our communities. Remember, you are not God, but neither is he or she. Many times I have heard hurting people say that some religious or spiritual figure in the past said hurtful things or behaved insensitively. Because of our false illusions that others may be essentially different from us, we may believe that an insight or comment from someone in a position of religious authority carries the authority of God. It probably doesn't. Mature spirituality results from self-awareness and the practice of surrender. If a religious messenger has hurt you, ask yourself why you should perceive them differently from other people. Many people speak with a tone of authority regarding spiritual messages, but the power given to the messenger or the message comes from us. We need not give power over our lives to anyone but God.

We are all going through the same process. Some of us have given more time and thought to spirituality than others, but surrender teaches us that we are all essentially the same. We know that every human person has limits. We are limited in our intellectual and physical capabilities. We are all vulnerable to emotions and uncertainty. Believing that someone else holds all the answers for us puts us in the unhealthy position of giving godly power to others—deifying them. Theologically speaking, that is idolatry.

Although many messengers in our lives can offer insights and hope, no one can do for us what we must do for ourselves. No one can walk the journey of surrender for you. No one can forgive for you. No one can accept those aspects of your life that you must learn to accept yourself. If you give a messenger undue power, you leave yourself open to the negative effects which may result from incorrect or unhealthy messages.

Listen to the insights of others. Accept those that feel right to you, those that seem to lead you to self-acceptance and the acceptance of others, those that lead you to love. Let go of the messages that do not resonate with your inner voice or your knowledge that God is love.

Consider what you are told by those with spiritual messages. Pray about it. And then take responsibility for those people and messages you decide to invite into the "car" of your life's journey. Some messengers may have some things you accept and other things you do not. Fine. We are not obligated to commit ourselves to the totality of another's insights. Sometimes we may hear a message which we choose to reject. Perhaps it feels emotionally violent to us or simply uncomfortable. Fine. Ignore it. You can come back to it later if you choose. Emotional violence does not come from the God who is love. Do not harm yourself in the name of the God of peace. If a religious leader has said something emotionally violent to you, respectfully feel sorry for him or her. People who are living out of their center of peace do not vent violence on others. The process of surrender will help you forgive them in time and allow you to see them realistically as just other humans on the planet.

Another way that some of us allow spiritual messengers to block the path of our own journey is by assuming that others have achieved a level of spiritual maturity of which we are not capable. This is always absolutely false. Since we are all essentially the same at our core, we have the same potential for holiness as anyone else. It is not helpful to look admiringly at someone else and think, "Well I could never pray like him, or love like they do or be as close to God as she is." Don't you believe it. If you want to pray more deeply, you can. If you want to love more fully, you can. Don't compare yourself to *your perception of others* and stop your own journey in frustration.

I have been shocked with comments from retreatants and workshop participants who sometimes say things like "Oh, I could never be as surrendered as you." A comment like that makes me sad. First, because it is made by someone who does not know me and has projected a false image on to me. Second, because the comment is simply not true. I once pointed out to someone that the audiotapes I had published on the topic of surrender were the result of my struggles to surrender, not of some preordained knowledge of it.

There are no levels of the spiritual life that are not open to all of us. We all have different gifts, it is true, but I know of no religious tradition that teaches that some people can follow spiritual principles and others should not. I love the tradition of keeping records of the lives of saints in the Catholic Church. Aside from their inspiration, I love the history and drama of human life as it is lived by those who want to know God. I have always considered learning about the saints to be a form of Catholic "witnessing" and I am disappointed that many young Catholics do not seem to know one saint from another. Still, I am concerned that the message some Catholics may have received from the lives of the saints is that some of us are meant for holiness and others are not.

"Get serious," I have heard people say in the midst of a religious discussion. "I am not a Mother Teresa you know." There was only one Mother Teresa, but she was the first to point out that there was nothing so unusual about being holy. "Holiness," she once said, "is simply the job for you and for me." And so it is. Mother Teresa was holy in her way, my next-door neighbor is holy in hers and we can be holy in ours. If we want to work through to our target of self-awareness, practice surrender and learn to love more, we will. If we don't want to, we won't. And if we don't want to but feel that we should, religion, religious institutions and religious messengers, when interpreted in healthy ways, can provide ready reasons to help keep us on the journey.

CHAPTER TEN

※

Suggested Exercises

There are a number of exercises that we can practice which will help us on the path to spiritual health and freedom through surrender. Some you may already practice. If so, keep it up. Most people report that the more they follow the exercises of their choice, the more surrender seems to become a part of their daily life. Like most spiritual principles, surrender must be worked at regularly—the way we work on our physical health through exercise. But we must remember to work cautiously. Just as we can expect to feel some discomfort after a physical workout, we can expect to feel uncomfortable or sad as we work through the steps to surrender. Similarly, severe pain—whether physical or emotional—means something is wrong: Stop what you're doing and seek the advice of a professional. If you begin to feel depressed by memories of the past or are seriously upset by your attempts to journey inward, it is important that you find a companion for your journey. But do not allow

laziness or inertia to keep you from your exercises. Find
one that works for you and stick with it!

Journaling

Writing down your thoughts and feelings each day is a
time-honored tool for personal growth and self-awareness.
It is a good idea to go back and read what you have written
in the past, noting any changes that may have occurred. I
usually recommend that journaling be done by hand rather
than with a computer—there is a connection between the
physical movement of your hand across the page and the
connection between body and spirit. For some of you,
though, computer keyboards are so much a part of daily
life that it may not make a significant difference.

The Daily Review

As you finish each day, consider what you have said, done
and felt, moment by moment. Do not write your thoughts
down, just reflect on how you have spent your time. Do not
judge yourself or others during your review. The point of
this exercise is simply to get to know ourselves better.

The daily review consists of rewinding the mental tapes
in our memories of each day. Nothing is considered unimportant in this review. I often ask people to start this review
with their first memory of the morning and then just watch
themselves going through the day. For example: There I am
brushing my teeth, now I am eating breakfast...now I am
talking to Susan in the hallway at work, she is annoying me
with her comments (no judgment here—just a review of the
facts)...now I am driving home. Someone just cut me off in
traffic. My reaction is instant and full of anger....

At first, this exercise may seem fruitless. Slowly
though, when we learn to just observe, not judge, we learn
a great deal about ourselves. We learn to see ourselves with
love, compassion and acceptance.

Open Hands Exercise

Sit comfortably with your hands open, palms resting upward on your lap. Close your eyes. Imagine the things in your life that you cling to most. Place the things you most want to hold on to—perhaps your money, reputation, family or friends—into your open hands. Now clasp your hands around them. Pull your hands into fists around them. Pull your fists tighter and tighter as you think of the things you most want to control or cling to. Clench your fists and feel the physical effort it takes to hold on. Hold on as tightly as you can until it becomes uncomfortable for you.

Now, slowly, begin to open your hands and talk to the person or thing you want to possess. You may tell a person that you love them but you recognize that you do not own them. You may tell a treasured material item that it gives you joy and you are grateful but you recognize that it is not part of your essence—your I am-ness—and that you could live in peace without it.

Continue your recognition of the truth (Tell yourself, "I do not own other people." "My material possessions are not part of my essence.") as you open your hands more and more. Notice the physical relief you experience as you stop straining to keep your fists tight. Finally imagine yourself, hands open, being engulfed by a brilliant warm light or comforting, loving arms holding you. You are practicing surrender and there may be some pain in saying good-bye before you experience the resurrection.

Like all exercises, this one does not instantly give dramatic results. It is just an exercise to help us be aware of what we are holding on to and how tightly. It can eventually help us let go of what we cling to. Remember, saying good-bye to your attempts to control or possess someone you love is not the same thing as saying good-bye to the relationship. You are only saying good-bye to your unhealthy lack of surrender in the relationship. This may be a frightening concept for some people, but ask yourself if, in truth, you are capable of possessing your loved one in a healthy way.

If you find this exercise too painful, do not force yourself. Try a more comfortable exercise and come back to this one later. Remember, no emotional violence, ever.

Picture Journaling

Instead of writing out your feelings in a journal, try drawing pictures. It does not matter if you are not a skilled artist, just pick up some colored pencils and begin. Draw whatever comes to mind. Use any colors you like. Date your pictures and collect them in a folder or notebook.

There are many ways to learn about ourselves through picture journaling. As we look at the pictures we have drawn we can notice the size of ourselves in our pictures. Are we drawn smaller than everyone else? Are we happy in our pictures? If we draw pictures of nature scenes or animals what do those things mean to us?

You may want to read *The Secret World of Drawings: Healing Through Art*, by Gregg M. Furth, as a guide.

Retreats

Retreats, days of quiet, workshops and spiritual direction are all very helpful tools for any spiritual undertaking. I recommend *Sanctuaries* by Jack and Marcia Kelly. It is an excellent guide to all of the monasteries and retreat houses in the United States that offer overnight lodgings. The sanctuaries they list are from a variety of religious traditions, and helpful information, such as cost and kind of retreats, is also listed.

Books

Spirituality is a popular topic in publishing. Bookstores and catalogs offer many wonderful works that can serve as guides for our spiritual path. My strongest recommendations regarding spiritual books is that you remember there is a difference between the message and the messenger. If a friend does not like the church a certain author is associated with, that does not negate the insight you may find helpful. Don't clutch or cling to one author or idea. Keep those hands open and assume the messenger is on the same journey. Also, remember to be a reflective and critical thinker when sorting through the many ideas these books offer. I have a house literally full of books. All of them have helped me to clarify, in some way, my interpretation of myself and my life. I particularly recommend the book, *Awareness* by Anthony DeMello, if you are interested in pursuing some of the principles of surrender.

A spiritual book discussion group is a good way to get yourself to read the books you have been meaning to, as well as share in the insights and reactions of others.

Pray

If you do not already do this, pray for at least a half-hour each day. There are many kinds of prayer and it is hard to find a better exercise for developing a disciplined and refreshing spiritual life. It is important to remember to listen in prayer as well as speak. There are many books on mantra meditation, centering prayer, the rosary as meditation and silent prayer. Try several forms of prayer and stick with the one that makes you most comfortable.

I recommend any books you choose (actually taking the time to review books and choose carefully is part of the process) on the topic of prayer. For me, even the books I decided I did not care for or agree with gave me insights that helped me form my preferences and opinions.

I especially recommend centering prayer. This ancient practice of praying by silently going inward is a great help for learning to know your center and become truly familiar with it. Also, check *Sanctuaries* for places near you which may offer workshops or retreats on this topic.

CONCLUSION

———————— ❀ ————————

The benefits of living a life of surrender far outweigh any challenges we may meet on the road toward it. Being free of the misery that a lack of surrender brings is truly a joy. The authentic spiritual surrender is always the result of a process, though, and trying to rush the process or demand it of others sets us in the opposite direction of surrender. Be kind to yourself. You are truly a sacred being. You may not feel that at this moment, but it is true nonetheless. At times the process toward surrender may seem to take us up stairs we thought we had already climbed. That is just part of the process. If you continue to be open and grow in self-awareness you will find the peace you seek.

Some of us may have a tendency to hold on to the idea of surrender just as we would a dream or goal we cannot let go of. Surrender is not a goal like planning to get a college degree. It is more like a lovely side-effect of growing in self-awareness.

If you decide that you want to grow in awareness of yourself, others and your world and you are open to dropping your illusions and seeing the truth—that is enough of a goal. There are specific things you can do, gently, to help yourself grow in this way. As you grow in awareness and acceptance you will find it is easier and easier to surrender the things that cause you misery. And, at the same time, while you get closer and closer to the very center of yourself you will come to know God in a way that is worth every step you have climbed or needed to reclimb.

When I was asked to write this book on surrender the publishers and I agreed on a date for the manuscript to be turned in. It seemed almost immediately after that a number of the parts of my life fell in on me with a crushing blow. I made a major professional decision which turned out to be a disaster. I had been warned by friends and professional mentors not to make the decision I did but I went ahead. Later, I was able to see that the decision was made out of a dream of mine and not a realistic assessment of the situation.

I had to deal with an abusive supervisor. One example of his behavior occurred when I called in sick one day. Although I told him I was extremely ill, he insisted I come in to work. I went in. That same evening I was taken to the hospital where I remained for a week with pneumonia. I honestly considered that week a relief from my difficult environment. My appeals to a higher supervisor felt even more abusive. Although the higher supervisor had assured me that if I had any difficulties with my supervisor I should come to her, when I followed her suggestion she, out of insecurity and an inability to know how to handle the problem (another woman was quitting because of the behavior of the supervisor) snapped at me, "I will not allow you to speak about the supervisor. I will not listen!"

Instead of thinking of the planks in my own eyes, accepting the fact that I could not change these two people or their behavior, and making constructive plans to find a healthier environment, I began to be overwhelmed by what I considered to be inappropriate and unprofessional behavior on the part of others. The specks in other people's eyes became my focus. I became angry and frustrated.

For years I had been peacefully following the path to surrender. Now there I was, a director of surrender workshops concentrating on the specks in the eyes of others. It seemed that all I could think of was how unprofessional "they" were and how very far they were from my expectations of them. If you find you have lost your way along the path to surrender, take heart—you will find your way again. When you feel yourself starting to experience misery, the spirit of God is calling you to get back to the surrender path. It can be done, and you will notice the positive change in your life when you return to the practice of surrender.

I experienced the difference surrender makes in the quality of life when, unlike my unhappy experience with my supervisor, I faced a different but equally painful situation with a longtime friend by surrendering and accepting what I could not change.

My friend began having problems with accepting some circumstances and people in her life. A normally kind person, she began to radiate anger toward everyone, including me. I tried to be understanding, waiting for the time to ask her what was wrong. When I asked her to speak about it, she refused. I accepted the fact that she did not want to speak about what was going on in her life. I also realized that it was not healthy for me to continue to allow her anger to affect my life in such a painful way. After three years of this awkward situation I let the friendship go, staying open to the possibility of renewing the relationship at another time.

For twenty years this friend and I shared our lives as only the best of friends can. I grieve the loss of her friendship, but I am not miserable about it. Unlike the me of some time ago I did not have any desire to try and make her behave in a way that suited me. I did not try to force her to talk. I did not get other friends involved. I have not felt betrayed over the unfairness of it all. I know her to be a loving and good person. If she wants to talk to me someday about this situation, she will. If she does not, I am grateful for the twenty years of friendship we shared. Another irony became clear to me. My friendship with this person and the insights she had were in part responsible for my ability to be so truly surrendered at the loss of the friendship. More gray in life. More mystery. I am truly at peace with what has transpired although I would have written the script in a different way if it were up to me. It is not up to me and I can accept that. As I said, the long slow process of surrender is worth the effort you invest.

One of the most important lessons in surrender I have learned involved the process of writing this book. Within the same period of time as my supervisor problem and the loss of an important friendship, I had a financial crisis; I had to borrow money to pay my basic bills. Then, for the first time in my life I experienced legal problems, something completely unfamiliar to me. Once again I had to borrow money to pay my attorney. The death of a family member and a friend (who was thirty-five years old) followed. My health failed, I became depressed and the surrender book was overdue.

I began to slowly clench my fists around my book on surrender! Old habits I was sure I had outgrown came back and seemed to haunt me. "What must my publisher think?" I fretted. I worried they would think me unprofessional or even lazy. I expected them to finally lose patience and cancel the book—I would not have blamed them. While trying to cope with the onslaught of problems that all came my way at the same time, more and more time went by and I asked again for more time from my publisher.

One night while having dinner with friends I expressed my concern about the book project. One of my friends pointed out the obvious irony of the surrender book needing to be surrendered. He suddenly began to speak with mock seriousness and took on a fake accent. I think he was trying to play Freud. "Hmmm, what are we to make of this prickly situation with the surrender book?" he asked. "Well, well, I can only conclude that the publishers of the surrender book are much more surrendered than the author!"

I broke into the deepest laughter of my life. The joke was funny, but my hearty laugh was only partly because of his humor. I was laughing the laughter of release. The joke had jolted me out of my old patterns of worry and into reality. It was a surrender breakthrough. If I was unable to spend time on the book and the publishers gave up waiting for me, that would be an understandable outcome and a reality I would have to face. I had to face my limits as a human being (another aspect of surrender) and accept the fact that I could not address all of my current life issues and write a book at the same time. Any wasted thoughts such as "Why did this all have to happen at the same time?" were set aside. I began to open my hands and accept my situation. And then I began to write.

For years I had been peacefully following the path of surrender. Now there I was, a director of surrender workshops concentrating on the specks in the eyes of others. It seemed that all I could think of was how unprofessional *they* were and how very far they were from my expectations of them. If you find you have lost your way along the path to surrender, take heart—you will find your way again. When you feel yourself start to experience misery, the spirit of God is calling you to get back to the surrender path. It *can* be done and you will notice the positive change in your life when you return to the practice of surrender.

A few weeks ago a former student of mine came to see me and show me her new baby. We had a delightful time playing with the baby and I enjoyed seeing the new mother so overwhelmed with love for her child. I first met her while she was in a class of mine that dealt with surrender. She had just been deserted by her boyfriend. He had pledged undying love for her, but the day he found out she was pregnant, he deserted her. I remember this young woman saying to me after class that "this surrender bull was fine for the classroom but would never work in real life." She began to cry, telling me her story, and said, "There is no way anyone could surrender what I am going through. I am pregnant, he won't talk to me and I feel hurt and angry and like a fool. I will never be able to get over this. I will never love anyone again. I will never be happy."

When I last saw her, I knew that she faced serious challenges, but she seemed happy. New life. Resurrection. As she prepared to leave after our visit she said to me, "You know, that surrender stuff really works doesn't it?"

"Yes," I told her, "It really does."